Marie Kondo's
Kurashi at Home

How to organize your space
and achieve your ideal life

Marie Kondo's Kurashi at Home

Marie Kondo

Photographs by Nastassia Brückin and Tess Comrie

Translated from the Japanese by Cathy Hirano

bluebird
books for life

CONTENTS

PREFACE

What matters most to you?

Tidying is far more than putting your house in order. It has the power to change your life.

What do you think changes most when you tidy?

For some people, tidying up improves their work performance or relationships, while for others, it leads to marriage or the discovery of something they really want to do.

But of all the effects of tidying, I think the most amazing is learning to like yourself.

Through the process of selecting what brings you joy and letting go of what doesn't, you develop your capacity to choose, to make decisions, and to take action, and this in turn develops your self-confidence.

By repeatedly asking yourself what sparks joy and what doesn't, you begin to see what matters most to you.

Liking yourself gives you emotional space and makes you want to enjoy each day to the fullest.

This book is for those of you who are learning to spark joy through the life-changing magic of tidying up.

A Dialogue
with Yourself

If you could make any dream come true, what would your ideal lifestyle be?

Exploring the answer to this question helps build the foundation for a life that sparks joy.

That's why I begin with every client by asking them to share their hopes and dreams. Their eyes shine as they describe a palatial house with lovely furniture in natural colours or a big kitchen where they can bake cakes. But before long reality starts to sink in, and the light in their eyes fades. 'I live in a tiny apartment', they'll say. 'How can I make a palace out of a room that's just 7.5 square metres? I guess I should be more realistic.'

On the surface, this seems like a perfectly logical conclusion, and to be honest, for a long time I wasn't quite sure how to respond. How could I ask my clients to compromise on their dreams? How could I tell someone who loves Renoir to decorate their one-room apartment with something 'more suitable', like Japanese woodblock prints, and just focus on keeping the space clean? That would never motivate them to tidy. The very thought would quench the least spark of joy.

When visualizing our ideal lifestyle, should we give our imagination free rein, or stick to what's possible? This is a tricky question - one I had to mull over for some time.

In Japanese, the word for 'lifestyle' is *kurashi*. As I pondered this word, I realized I didn't know exactly what it meant. Looking it up in the *Daijisen* dictionary of Japanese terms, I discovered an interesting fact.

According to this source, it means 'the act of living; spending each day; daily life; making a livelihood'. The verb *kurasu* means 'to pass one's time until sunset; to spend one's day'. In other words, the ideal kurashi simply means the ideal way of spending our time, and therefore is separate from the 'ideal home'.

This realization reminded me of my university days when I lived in Tokyo with my parents. Even though I had my own little room, which in Japanese cities is a huge luxury, I was always full of ideals and aspirations. I dreamed of having a bigger room, a cuter kitchen, a little garden on the balcony, nicer curtains on the windows, and so on. But the kitchen was my mother's territory, which I was forbidden to change without permission, and my room didn't even have a window, let alone a balcony.

But this gap between my dreams and reality didn't bother me. I used to boast about how much I loved my room. The reason I loved it was because it was my own space, a place where I could enjoy my ideal lifestyle, whether that meant relaxing before bed with aromatherapy, listening to my favourite classical music, or placing a small vase with a single flower on my bedside table.

In other words, the ideal lifestyle refers to what we do, not to where we live.

Once my clients finish tidying up their homes, very few of them consider moving or completely redecorating afterward. Often the biggest change they describe is how they spend their time at home. Through these changes, they come to love the space in which they live, regardless of whether it matches their ideal.

Even if you can't move to a new house or apartment, you can still change your lifestyle. You just need to live as if your space *is* your ideal home. That's really the point of tidying up. So, when imagining your ideal lifestyle, think concretely about what you'd like to do and how you'd like to spend your time at home.

Oddly enough, once they've finished tidying and have realized their ideal lifestyle, many of my clients actually end up with the house – and even the furnishings – of their dreams. I can't count the times I've heard my clients say things like, 'Two years after tidying we moved into a house exactly like the one I imagined.' Or 'Someone gave me the kind of furniture I'd always wanted.' This is one of the many strange and wonderful effects of tidying that I've witnessed through my work.

Whether you believe it or not is up to you. But if you're going to imagine your ideal lifestyle, why not go all out?

Have you given up on your ideal home?

Although changing the way we spend our time can bring us closer to our ideal lifestyle, I'm not suggesting that we give up our vision of the ideal home and substitute something more 'realistic'. That would negate the whole concept of sparking joy through tidying. So how can you achieve the living space of your dreams? Is it possible, for example, to redo a typical one-room, tatami-mat Japanese apartment in rococo style? I once thought something like that would be inconceivable, but in fact even this can be done.

One of my favourite books is *Fashion Encyclopedia of Akihiro Miwa* (published by Shueisha, Inc.), in which Miwa, a Japanese celebrity, presents the one-room apartment where he lived in his youth. Although the space was only about 10 square metres, the interior was gorgeous. Miwa carpeted the straw tatami mats with plush-covered cardboard, covered the sliding closet doors with checkerboard cloth, and adorned them with photos of famous actresses. Handmade pink curtains graced the windows, while the dresser, record player, and other items were transformed with paint and ribbons. In the photographs, the space resembles a room in a luxurious European palace rather than a traditional Japanese-style room.

'You don't have to move or spend lots of money to make your home chic and charming. Instead, redecorate it with a little creative intelligence and innovation.' These words from Miwa's book continue to encourage and inspire me.

I first read the book when I was at university. Miwa was invited to be the guest speaker at our university festival, and as a member of the student newspaper club, I was given the opportunity to interview him.

I had never met anyone like him. He spritzed the meeting room with rose perfume before we gathered and spoke in the most eloquent and courteous language. I was awed by his presence, an experience I will never forget. *So, this is what they mean by the 'real thing',* I thought.

Although still a student, I'd already begun working as a tidying consultant and had noticed that the atmosphere of every home seemed to match the person who inhabited it. Curious to see what kind of places Miwa had lived in, I discovered his book.

Since then, I've observed the lifestyles of many people, but the common factor that I most admire in their homes is certainly not spaciousness. Nor is it the luxury of the furnishings. Rather, it's the person's longing to live in a certain kind of space. That longing is evident in the way they spare no effort to create their dream, seeking out and choosing only the things they truly love, right down to the most insignificant storage item. It's there in their passion for remaking existing items and in the respect and care with which they treat their home and belongings.

The word *longing* may sound overly dramatic, but the refusal to compromise when it comes to realizing their vision makes such people passionate about their home and creates a deep affection for it.

That's why I urge you not to give up on having the house of your dreams. Never hold back when imagining your ideal home and lifestyle. Search the web and browse through books and magazine features on home interiors to collect photos of gorgeous dwellings or even attractive hotel rooms from around the world. Spend time just admiring them, while picturing in your mind the kind of living space that would spark joy for you. And don't discourage yourself by comparing the home of your dreams to your current reality.

When I was much younger, I used to gaze wistfully at photos of the homes of glamorous people, envying their lives, convinced I could never have such a house myself. These thoughts made me so uptight that I couldn't feel the joy those pictures naturally inspired in me. Looking at photos of beautiful homes is actually a great way to learn what kind of living space sparks joy for you and to hone your sensitivity to joy. It's important to think positively, so let go of the tendency to compare yourself to others or put yourself down. Instead look for hints in your instinctive reactions to the things you see, whether it's the colour of a wall or a design idea you'd like to try.

Give yourself the freedom to imagine your own personal 'wouldn't it be nice if' living space, and let your heart brim with joy.

Don't worry. With a little effort and inventiveness, you can transform the space you're currently living in.

What do you really want to put in order?

So, tell me. Why did you decide to tidy up?

When asked this question, many people focus on their desire to declutter the space in front of them. 'I want to organize my home', they say. Or 'I want to cut down on the time it takes to find things'.

There's nothing wrong with these responses. After all, the task of tidying your home is a physical one.

But if you want to tap into the life-changing magic of tidying up, there are a few points you should consider before you start.

I always begin my tidying lessons by asking these questions:

Were you good at tidying as a child?

What kind of work do you do?

Why did you choose your job?

How do you spend your days off?

When did you first get involved in such activities?

What do you enjoy doing most?

I might devote as much as an hour to these subjects with a client, even though some of them appear to be irrelevant. I don't ask these questions just out of curiosity. Each is a key piece in making the tidying process smoother.

There often comes a point while a client is organizing a particular category, such as clothes or books, when their pace drops and they struggle to make progress. Some can't bring themselves to discard any clothes, while others may feel impelled to hang on to more detergent than they need. Like a knot in a muscle, these points represent blocks in the tidying process.

A block in a particular area of tidying invariably corresponds to a block in some aspect of the person's life, such as their relationships or work. For some, the root cause may be that they're bored with their job. For others, it may be that they're unable to forgive their mother for something in the past or need to discuss something with their spouse or partner but haven't had the courage to bring it up.

The questions I ask at the beginning are designed to loosen up these knots in my clients' lives – knots they may not even realize exist. This isn't a time to offer them advice or think up solutions. I simply ask the questions and let them respond.

Even a little reflection on aspects of our lives that we haven't yet put in order can dramatically accelerate the tidying process. It helps us see why we resist discarding certain items and recognize what we're really attached to. As a result, tidying progresses at a deeper level.

How we approach our possessions, relationships, work, and way of life is all interconnected. This is why it's more effective to tackle blocks from both angles: our possessions and our inner selves.

Tidying up means dealing with all the 'things' in your life. So, what do you really want to put in order? Take a moment to consider this question one more time.

The KonMari Method

If you've read any of my other books, you're familiar with my KonMari Method of tidying – you may have already given it a try yourself! The basis of the KonMari Method is to go through your belongings all in one go, proceeding category by category in the following order:

clothes

books

papers

komono (miscellaneous items)

sentimental items

Start by gathering all the items from a category in one spot. Then touch each item to see if it sparks joy for you. If it does, keep it with confidence. If it doesn't, let it go. This process has the power to change your mindset so thoroughly that you'll never revert to clutter. That's why I call it a 'tidying festival'. It's a major life-transforming event, which is cause for celebration. It's also an opportunity to thank and honor those items that once sparked joy for you but have served their purpose.

But how do you know what sparks joy and what doesn't? Just looking at something won't do the trick – you have to pick it up and hold it in your hands. When you touch something that brings you joy, you'll know almost instinctively.

You might feel a tingling of excitement, a bubbly happiness, or an easing of tension. You're tidying up because you want to live a happy, fulfilling life, so it's only natural to ask yourself if the things you want to keep spark joy. Thinking about what you want to keep in your life is the same as thinking about how you want to live your life.

As you progress through your tidying journey, you'll be able to see more clearly what you need to keep and what you should let go, what you want to continue doing and what you should stop. It takes a lot of courage to make such decisions, but have faith in yourself. Once you've learned to choose only what you love most, you'll be able to live a life that sparks joy. No matter what anyone says, keep what you've picked with confidence. When you cherish the things you keep, you live surrounded by treasures. Taking good care of the things you love means that you are listening to and taking care of yourself.

Is tidying stressing you out?

'I didn't get any tidying done today.'

'I'll never finish at this rate.'

'I've got to get rid of more stuff.'

'I simply must declutter.'

Are you feeling overwhelmed by tidying?

Are you obsessed with getting rid of things, or panicking because you think your house will never truly be organized? Judging from the messages I receive, many people feel this way. And that's a shame.

Tidying should give us the freedom to savour each day, but if we forget why we're tidying, if we lose sight of the lifestyle we want or of where we are at in the tidying process, we begin to neglect our sense of joy.

If this has happened to you, there's no need to panic.

When it comes to other things than tidying, I often find myself in the very same state. Although I love my work, sometimes I pack my schedule so tightly I feel frazzled or am overcome with anxiety, even though my relationships are fulfilling. And occasionally, I'll get upset about things that would ordinarily never bother me. After our first child was born, I initially strove to be a mother who could balance childrearing, homemaking, and work with ease. Instead, I ended up exhausted. As a tidying professional, I sometimes pressure myself with expectations that my house should always be in order.

At times like these, however, I have learned to pause and remind myself to let go of perfection.

If you find you've run out of time or emotional space, I recommend letting go of something. The trick is to decide what your bottom line is on any given day. In my case, it's that my children are healthy and happy and that I don't get worn out. If the toys are scattered about but I'm too tired to deal with them right then, I remind myself that it's okay to go to bed without putting them away. Conversely, if the mess has gone on so long it's starting to bother me, I rearrange my schedule and set aside a day to put things back in order.

When I feel so overwhelmed that I'm in danger of losing myself, I take time to write down everything that's weighing on me.

My husband and I consult daily about our work schedules and tasks, jotting down what we need to do that day and the next in quite a bit of detail. We even include such minute chores as loading the washing machine and putting clothes in the dryer. The list ensures I don't forget what needs doing, and checking off each item once it's completed gives me a sense of achievement. If some items are left unchecked at the end of the day, that's fine. It feels better to have a clear idea of what still needs to be done than to have a nagging anxiety that I've forgotten to do something or a sense of frustration every time I pass a room and see it needs tidying.

Writing things down not only helps me with scheduling, but also with sorting out my feelings. I adopted this habit many years ago. Whenever I found it hard to stay calm, when I just couldn't seem to forgive someone, or when ideas came bubbling up one after the other, demanding my

attention, I would sit down at my trusty writing desk, which dated back to my university days, face my computer screen, and pour out my thoughts in a flood of words, secure in the knowledge that no one but me would ever read them.

If you're having trouble identifying your ideals, if you've hit a block, or if a jumble of words is teasing your mind, try using a pen and paper instead of a computer. You can even seek out a different spot, such as a quiet café or park bench, where you can write without interruption.

In my case, I might write in a notebook, a diary, or on random pieces of paper, depending on the purpose. For jotting down thoughts that don't spark joy, I find that the best kind of paper is the blank side of a flyer or other printed material destined for the recycle bin. That way I feel no compulsion to write neatly, unlike when using a proper notebook. While I don't bother to keep a stock of such paper on hand, it's always easy to find some when I need it.

Regardless of which method you choose, you're bound to discover in the words that flow onto the page feelings you weren't aware of and the reasons behind them. At times they may make you blush with embarrassment or glow with pleasure. It's a bit like gathering all your possessions in one spot during a tidying festival, don't you think?

So, if tidying starts to feel stressful, take a break. Make yourself a cup of tea and pause to contemplate your lifestyle and the things around you. Remember: The true purpose of tidying is not to cut down on your possessions or declutter your space. The ultimate goal is to spark joy every day and lead a joyful life.

Have you set a deadline for tidying up?

Tidy up quickly, all in one go.

This is key to the KonMari Method, but people often ask me, 'How long is "quickly"?'

The answer depends on the person.

Some people can finish within a week, whereas others need three months or even half a year. The important thing is to decide when we want to finish. Without a clear deadline, it's human nature to put things off indefinitely.

Although I'm embarrassed to admit it, in my case, I tend to put off writing. Take my first book, for instance. The project began with a meeting at the publisher's office. I expounded on the theme of tidying for a couple of hours, explaining to the editor the right way to go about it and how it could make life so much better. He seemed totally convinced and suggested I start by writing down whatever came into my mind. So, I began without a firm deadline.

When I got home, the flow of passionate ideas seemed to have dried up. Tidying is my life. Having to sit down in front of a computer and tap away at the keyboard was torture. I found one excuse after another to avoid doing it.

Two weeks later, I sent an email to my editor apologizing for not having been able to write a single word. I had never felt so miserable.

After that, I asked the editor to give me short-term deadlines, or I made my own and announced them to him. To be honest, I still tend to leave writing to the last minute, but at least I no longer put it off indefinitely.

Unlike me, tidying is not your profession, which is precisely why you should set a deadline for it if you haven't already.

If you find it hard to stay motivated on your own, try telling your friends or family. You could even post a declaration on social media, announcing your intention to finish tidying by the end of the year. It may not be as binding as a work deadline, but the thought that people will be wondering how it's going will motivate you to get started and help you see it through.

One of my clients finished tidying up with astonishing speed because her deadline was the end of her maternity leave. Her hands moved so fast they blurred as she murmured 'This sparks joy' and 'Thank you'. When there were only a few days left and the clock was ticking, she insisted that we have lunch at a curry restaurant a fifteen-minute walk away. 'Once my leave ends, I won't be able to eat here', she said. Privately, I worried that the lunch might waste precious time, but she still managed to finish tidying up.

Having a firm deadline helps us focus and makes us more productive. That's human nature.

So, when do you want to complete your tidying festival? Flip open your diary and write 'Last Day of Tidying' on that day. Yes, I mean now.

When will you start tidying?

When will you start? When will you finish?

Although these questions sound similar, they are two very different questions. This is obvious from my clients' responses. Their faces glow as they tell me when they plan to finish. 'By New Year's Eve. My goal is to become a brand-new me and get married next year!' 'By my birthday! And when I'm done, I'm going to celebrate. I'll buy myself a bouquet of flowers and a special tea set and sit back with a cup of tea.' They boldly write 'Last Day of Tidying!' into their diaries. Their eyes sparkle as they describe the life they'll lead when they're done.

But when I ask them, 'When are you going to start?' their responses go something like this:

'Umm . . . well, all my weekends this month are full. And I was thinking of traveling during the summer holidays . . .'

'Let's see . . . well, I have this day free, but I'm going out drinking the night before, so I'll probably be too tired. *Hmmm*. And this day I might go out in the evening too.'

They cast apologetic glances at me as their eyes dart back and forth between me and their diaries.

The reason is clear: Thinking about finishing means dreaming about the future, whereas thinking about starting is for real. It makes perfect sense that deciding when to start is much harder.

Sometimes I see how my clients mark the dates for my lessons on their wall calendars. It's not so bad when they write things like, 'Tidying lesson! You can do it!' But it's rather disconcerting to see a large triangle with an exclamation mark inside or even a skull and crossbones. It makes me feel more like a hazard than a tidying expert. When I ask why they did this, they say it's because they're uncertain what's in store for them or because they know it's going to be 'do or die'. At times, their expressions are so intense I almost drop my rubbish bags.

For most people, getting started takes commitment and effort.

Of course, some people jump right in as soon as they get the urge to tidy up, checking which clothes spark joy without a second thought. But such

people are few and far between. The majority have to pore over their calendars, looking for possible dates. They rearrange their schedules, take paid holidays, or cancel appointments to make time. Often they will stay up tidying until 2:00 in the morning or even all night before a lesson. When I see their pale, sleep-deprived faces the next day, I have to restrain myself from saying, 'But you've had a whole month since the last lesson! Why didn't you start sooner?' Yet I myself invariably do an all-nighter when I have a manuscript due. I guess putting things off until the last minute is not so unusual!

That's why I encourage you to take the plunge now if you haven't already. Set aside your excuses about being busy for a moment and consult your diary one more time. I promise: There is always an end to tidying. And you're not alone. Plenty of people the world over are tackling tidying just like you.

So, when are you going to start?

Ask Marie

My partner's messy, and I can't keep my home tidy. Help!

If you live with someone else, such as your partner or family, the trick to keeping your place tidy is to make sure everything has an easily identifiable spot where it belongs. The most important point is to make it clear at a glance where each thing goes. If this is unclear or changes frequently, or if you yourself aren't even sure where something belongs, trying to get others to tidy up will be a long, hard road.

I recommend identifying which spaces you can have total control over and tidying them thoroughly. This could be your closet, a bookcase, or a room or designated area for pursuing your personal interests, but they should be spaces you can always keep tidy. By starting with these areas, you can get a feel for the basics of tidying and gain some peace of mind. Then, from that mindset, you can begin thinking about the spaces you share with others. Many people do the opposite: they try to fix spaces that belong to others first. If you're one of these people, stop to ask yourself, 'Is *my* space in perfect order?'

It's hard to change someone else. But we *can* change ourselves. As the goal of tidying up is to create a lifestyle that sparks joy, it's important to confront ourselves and put our own space in order. If you live with someone else, close your eyes to any mess they make during your tidying process. You can only experience the pleasure of tidying when you have taken the time to put your own life in order.

Once you've discovered that tidying is an enjoyable experience instead of a painful, exasperating chore – once you can really translate that concept into action – your energy will change. As a result, those who live with you will gradually begin to tidy up too. Tidying, it seems, can cause a chain reaction, something I have witnessed frequently.

The timing of this change depends on the person. For some, it happens as soon as they begin tidying up. For others, it may not happen until half a year after they finish. But invariably, the people they live with start tidying up of their own accord.

The relationship between tidying and our home and family is neither short-term nor superficial, so it's important to remember that you're creating a lifestyle that sparks joy with your entire household. Seek opportune moments with those you love for sharing ideas about what that lifestyle might look like.

What if everything sparks joy?

If you truly feel that everything you own sparks joy, that's wonderful! In that case, let's change the premise of tidying. There's no need to think about throwing anything away. What matters is that you cherish every item you own and feel comfortable and happy in your home. If everything still sparks joy even after you've tidied up, that's just fine.

Instead, I recommend brushing up your storage. Focus on how to store your things in a way that brings you delight. For example, identify the categories more clearly and choose thoughtfully where to keep each item. Store things upright and arrange them to inspire delight each time you open a drawer. Take pleasure in exploring the best way to store all the things you love and cherish.

I've met many people who insist they can't throw anything away because 'it all sparks joy', only to discover that this is not quite true. After following the KonMari Method of gathering all their possessions, one category at a time, and touching each item, they realize that some things no longer give them a thrill – even items in a favourite collection. Although the number of these items might be very few, it's the process of reassessing what we love and what we don't that's important. Only through this process can we create the conditions in which all our things really and truly spark joy. If you believe everything sparks joy when you've only dipped your toe into the tidying process instead of plunging right in, you may not have a full grasp of what you own.

A good indicator that all your things spark joy is if you feel happy and content whenever you're at home.

TWO

A Dialogue with Your Home and Possessions

This chapter will help you delve into your relationship with your home and possessions. Reflecting on the memories and feelings your things inspire will deepen your understanding of tidying.

If your home had a personality, what kind of person would it be?

Each home has its own personality and character.

Many of my clients look puzzled when I say this, but having visited countless homes day after day, year after year, I'm sure this is true, even though I can't explain why.

Some are feminine and others masculine; some are young and vibrant, others serene and mature. Some are vivacious and others quiet. Some conjure up vivid images. The character and communication style of each is different.

My first task when beginning a new series of tidying lessons is to get to know my client's home. My method is simple: I say 'Hello', and ask it to support us during the tidying process. The feeling I get in response gives me an idea of its personality. I'm not trying to analyze or categorize homes into types. I'm simply trying to get a feel for what each one is like, the same way we can sense a person's nature through a conversation.

You may wonder if knowing the personality of a home is useful. In fact, it's no use at all. But if I make a good connection with a home from the start, it will often nudge me in the right direction when I'm looking for solutions, such as how to store things in a certain area.

I've come to the conclusion that homes are essentially very kind. If something at work is bothering me, my house seems to wrap me in a gentle embrace on my return, and often the next morning my problems have disappeared.

Why not try greeting your home and see what happens?

Can your things breathe?

Clothes jammed into the closet. Books and magazines stacked in random piles on the floor. Komono on top of a bookcase or dresser.

Are there things in your house that are gasping for air? Listen closely to what each one is trying to tell you. If you're wondering how that can be done, try the 'solo performance' method. First, turn off any music, then take a good look around the room. If a particular object catches your eye, try imagining what it's feeling and become its voice. Say whatever words pop into your mind. For example, 'This weight is crushing me,' or 'Please put me back in the drawer,' or even, 'I quite like it this way. It's very liberating.' By pretending to be each thing, you'll start to understand it.

By the time you've taken on the roles of ten or twenty items and are really getting into acting, you will probably have made some important discoveries. Perhaps some of your things are telling you how they want to be stored, while others are announcing that their role in your life is over. You might even receive a flash of inspiration about something you need to accomplish tomorrow or what you want to do in life.

Everything you own wants to help you. So, think about how you can make the space for each one more comfortable. This is the essence of planning storage. Storage is the sacred ritual of returning things to where they belong. To do it right, you need to put yourself in each thing's shoes. I hope that by doing so, you'll see that tidying is not a set of storage techniques, but rather a process of enhancing your communication with the things in your life.

Of all your belongings, which have you cherished the longest?

Take a good look at all the things you own. Which ones have you cherished the longest? Look for something you keep nearby that's always in use, not something you had forgotten and just now realized was there.

For me, it's my sewing box – it's a wooden one with drawers. It was a Christmas present from my parents when I was in first grade. The metal fastener on the lid broke once and was repaired, leaving holes in odd places, but I love the colour of the wood and the pattern of carved flowers. At one time it held my makeup, but now I'm using it for sewing again.

My sewing box has witnessed all the joys and sorrows in my life. Although it's a little embarrassing to think it has seen me at my worst as well as at my best, it's also reassuring, like being with a good friend I can confide anything to. I feel perfectly at ease in its presence, confident that it accepts me just the way I am, flaws and all.

When you find something like that, pick it up and hold it, polish it affectionately, and ask it to keep supporting you. That it has stayed with you all this time proves that it has been watching over you with care. Isn't it time to return the favour?

I believe that when we consciously cherish something precious, we deepen our relationship with it, and this in turn deepens our bonds with

other things in our lives, bringing out the best in them and in ourselves.

Are there things you love and keep without realizing why?

When I ask my clients if they've ever felt the hand of destiny in finding a particular item, they usually give me one of two responses: that they felt an instantaneous shock of recognition the moment they laid eyes on something, as if a gong had sounded in their head, or they came to a slowly dawning realization that they're still using something after twenty years. I find this latter type intriguing.

When I question my clients about their first encounter with such items, their answers seem surprisingly nonchalant. 'I don't remember when I got it,' they say. Or 'I bought it on a whim.' I first noticed this type of response when I was still a student, not long after I began my tidying business. Influenced by TV dramas and manga, I expected that true attraction to anything must mean 'love at first sight'. I was surprised to learn this wasn't always the case.

It made me wonder if I already owned something that had been destined for me, but I hadn't yet noticed. Upon reflection, I realized that in fact I did – my diary.

I began using a particular kind of diary while still in junior high and continued to use it for most of my 20s – over fifteen years. My old school friends were surprised I was still using the same type. It was pocket-sized, about as big as a cassette tape. Its design was extremely simple, with just one page for each month's schedule. But the colour printing and comical illustrations for each month definitely sparked joy for me.

Now I use a larger diary because my schedule is simply too complex to fit into one so small, but my first diary was such a perfect match for me at the time that I'm convinced my encounter with it was fate. Even so, I have no memory of when I first found it.

This made me think that our first impressions of something don't always indicate that it's destined to be in our lives. Wondering if the same holds true when people first meet their 'soul mate', I began casually asking my clients how they met their partners, using a sentimental item found in the back of a closet or drawer as an excuse. A surprising number responded with things like, 'We just happened to work at the same place', 'Before I realized it, we were always together,' or 'He didn't really make much impression on me at the time.' Many of them added, 'But it feels so natural to be together.'

My relationship with my husband, Takumi, was also the slow-budding kind. I met him at a job-hunting networking event for students when we were both in university, and afterward we continued to meet casually,

maybe once or twice a year, for about eight years.

It seems to me that the depth of our connection with certain people or things depends more on whether we're well matched than on the impact they make during our first encounter.

Did one of your things click the instant you saw it?

Then there are those things that click the moment we set eyes on them. We recognize instantly that they're a perfect match for us. They seem to have been made just for us or to be crying out, 'Take me home!'

Judging from what people tell me, these items are diverse: it might be something you carry or wear, such as a white leather bag or a pair of earrings with lovely blue stones, or it could be a mug, a sofa, or even a plant. Some of my clients make all their purchases based on whether something clicks, but even those who haven't reached that level of identifying what sparks joy have usually felt 'love at first sight' in response to something.

For me, it was a painting that I found during a trip with my family when I was in college. I just happened to wander into a shop and discovered a painting inspired by *Alice in Wonderland* in the back. The composition was so perfect that I stared at it spellbound. For the next thirty minutes, I agonized over whether to buy it, going in and out of the shop until I finally made up my mind. When I got home and hung it on my wall, it felt as though my room was now complete. I had never experienced something like that before. Yet despite this fateful encounter, I actually let the painting go. A client told me that her daughter loved *Alice in Wonderland*, and I decided to give it to her. Five years had passed since I bought it, and for some reason I thought its role in my life was finished. Once it was gone, however, something odd happened: the picture kept appearing in my dreams.

At first I thought this was just a coincidence, but it happened almost every day. A week later, my mother called me. 'Marie,' she said. 'You still have that picture of Alice, don't you?'

'What? Um . . .'

'I've been dreaming about it every night for the last few days. It must be very important to you, so take good care of it, will you?'

After she hung up, I decided my reoccurring dream was no accident. I phoned my client. When she heard what had happened, she was more than happy to return the picture. I still have no idea what my dream was trying to tell me, but immediately afterward, I reached a turning point in my work, and things began to move ahead quite smoothly. It was as if that picture were watching over me.

I've kept it with me ever since, taking it with me when I got married and when we moved to America. Even more than joy, it inspires a profound sense of peace and security in me every time I look at it.

Things that click only come to us when the timing is right. And even if we part with them temporarily, they will always come back. Such encounters are truly magical, don't you think?

THREE

Visualize
Your Ideal
Home

In this chapter, you will visualize your ideal home, one space at a time. I introduce examples for each space from my own or my clients' lifestyles to help you imagine what your own ideal might be.

Your entranceway is the face of your home, its most sacred spot.

The entranceway to our home should inspire a sigh of relief and contentment as we walk through the door, making us want to announce, 'I'm home!' Clean and neat, it should make guests feel uplifted and warmly welcomed. That's my image of the ideal entranceway.

For example, the floor is kept immaculate, and all shoes except one pair for each family member are stowed neatly in the cupboard or closet. The delicate fragrance of essential oils or incense drifts in the air, and the eye is drawn to a point of joy, such as a tasteful entrance mat, a favourite picture or postcard, or a single flower in a vase. This focal point changes to reflect the season, whether it be New Year's, autumn, or the winter holidays.

The entranceway to one client's home made a particularly strong impression on me. Taking center stage was a model ship her husband had made, and beside it she had displayed tasteful ikebana arrangements made with seasonal flowers. After the couple's children grew up and moved away, they gradually began to add decorative touches to their home. They have now made it a custom to greet their house every day. I still remember their smiling faces as they told me, 'It brings us so much pleasure to come home and open the front door.'

Your entranceway is the face of your home, its most sacred spot. The key here is to keep decoration simple.

What do you want to see when you open the door? What would spark more joy as you step inside? A particular fragrance? A special accent or ornament? Maybe you'd like to reorganize and simplify the process of entering your house by adding benches or taking a different approach to shoe storage.

The Entrance to Your Home Is Like the Gate to a Shrine

I wipe the floor of my entranceway with a well-rung damp rag. Although this may seem like an unnecessary bother, I recommend wiping or mopping the entranceway if you seek a lifestyle that sparks joy.

I started doing this while I was still in senior high. Although I've forgotten the title, I was inspired by a book on feng shui, which advised that wiping your entranceway floor each day increases your good fortune. The home entrance, it explained, is like the face of the homeowner. Keeping it clean and bright raises the prestige of your house and attracts good luck.

I took these words quite literally at first. *I see! So this is my dad*, I thought, imagining myself wiping his face as I scrubbed away. This seemed rather disrespectful, however, so instead I decided to empty my thoughts of everything but polishing the entranceway.

I was surprised to see how filthy the rag always got, even though I wiped the entranceway daily. *Look at all the dirt we pick up in a single day,* I thought. *Is this what it means to be human – to shake off the dust each day at home and reset ourselves for another day at work?* I must have looked rather comical as I knelt in my high school uniform, rag in hand, pondering the meaning of life.

When I began my tidying business, I shared with my clients what the book had said about cleaning the entranceway. 'Oh, I get it!' one of them remarked. 'It's like the gateway to a Shinto shrine.' She was right! I once worked part-time as a shrine maiden, and we were taught that walking through the shrine gate cleanses away defilement and misfortune. Similarly, when we pass through the entrance to our home, it removes all the grime we collect during the day.

Another client made the observation that cleaning her entranceway helps wipe away feelings of guilt and shame. She realized that seeing dirt in her entranceway had been making her feel like a failure. (For some reason, this habit tends to inspire philosophical insights like these.)

Keeping our entrance spotless can give us the confidence that comes from knowing we have nothing to hide. At the same time, it instills in us a respect for our home as a sacred place. Perhaps this small space is really a place for purifying our minds. If so, then it makes sense that keeping our entranceways clean will increase our good fortune. In Japan, people say that 'happiness comes through the front door'. Wiping the entrance floor makes the air flowing through the house seem lighter. Would you like to turn your home into a power spot, just like a Shinto shrine? If so, make a habit of wiping your entranceway every day.

Make your living room a space that fosters conversation.

Your living room is a place for connecting with family, friends, and even yourself. It can serve as a space for both relaxation and lively conversation. In our living room, we've made a play space to spend time with our children before or after dinner. We read to them and enjoy watching them dance about and sing. This space helps our family create moments of joy. We've also set aside a spot beside the TV for photos, made a special nook to display our children's crafts, and created a corner for seasonal decorations, which we change every so often to mark occasions like Christmas.

While the children are at school, our living room becomes a precious place for me to relax with a cup of tea. From the remote control to newspapers and magazines, everything has a designated place, and the room is always neat and tidy. You can use hidden storage, such as cabinets or compartments in your coffee table, or keep items together on trays that spark joy. For remotes, use narrow baskets to keep them out of sight for a tidier look. I like to adorn the living room space with a vase of pretty flowers, and a favourite house plant stands in one corner. 'You're looking very well,' I say each time I water it. 'Thank you for keeping the air fresh and clean.' Depending on my mood, I'll put on some classical music or jazz and relax on the sofa to give myself a break from work.

People who tell me their living room is the place that really sparks joy will often create their own little art galleries, selecting items that impart beauty such as paintings, lovely objects, or seasonal flowers. One client who loved things that sparkle placed sun catchers in the window, large

crystals and glass ornaments on the TV console, and a solar-powered rainbow maker on one wall. Her living room was spellbinding, filled all day with soft, rainbow-coloured reflections.

For me, the ideal living room is a well-ventilated space with a favourite sofa and coffee table and an atmosphere that fosters joyful conversations.

What kind of living room fits your lifestyle? What place within it or what decoration would serve as a focal point? How can you organize the items in the room so they all have designated places?

A good kitchen makes cooking fun!

I spend a significant amount of my day in the kitchen. It's not only where I cook for my family, but also where we eat together. The children like to watch me cook. Even when they're playing in the playroom, as soon as I start cooking, they'll appear and ask to help. I think they're drawn to the kitchen because they see I'm having fun. I ask them to beat the eggs, cut the vegetables, or empty the dishwasher. Our time together in the kitchen is also a precious opportunity for conversation.

My rule is never to keep anything on the counter near the sink or stove, where it might get splattered with oil or water. This makes it easy to immediately wipe the counter and keep it clean. I keep the number of pots and pans I use to a minimum and choose ones that are easy to use and care for.

Kitchen utensils such as ladles and cooking chopsticks are kept in one spot. Other items are divided and stored by simple categories, such as dishes, cooking tools, and seasonings, so they are close at hand when needed. Bagged pantry goods, such as dried foods, are stored upright, and I check the expiration dates frequently to be sure to use them up before they go bad. Refrigerated groceries are stored so they can all be seen at a glance, to minimize expired food remaining in the fridge. Food storage containers of the same design can create a tidier look. It can be a lot of fun to search for and gradually collect canisters or other kitchen komono you really love.

After completing her tidying festival, one of my clients proudly showed me a wooden paper towel holder, a birthday gift from her husband.

'Before, I was always racing out to buy the latest kitchen gadget,' she said. 'But now I realize that changing even one item to something I really love can make every day feel special.'

My ideal kitchen is clean, makes cooking fun, and lets me enjoy time with my family.

What do you want to reduce or add to make your kitchen easier to use? Are there any cooking utensils or tools you want to upgrade to make cooking more fun, or any tired-out dish towels, kitchenware, or other things that you want to replace?

Don't just focus on the practical – give your workspace a playful touch.

A workspace where ideas and inspiration flow and where work moves along quickly and smoothly is wonderful, isn't it? Whether you have your own separate office or work at a desk in a room with others, let's consider what kind of space is ideal for working in.

Of course, the ideal is to have your desktop clear, books and documents neatly arranged on the bookshelves according to categories of your own choosing, and no excess papers piling up, so you can tell at a glance where everything is. All documents, and even pens and stationery items in the desk drawers, should be stored upright so that everything can be seen instantly when the drawer is opened. Tidying our physical spaces like this can also inspire us to adopt new habits that bring us joy.

One of my clients expanded her tidying festival from her home to her workplace. She starts each day by wiping her desk with a dust cloth and spritzing her workspace with peppermint or lavender, depending on her mood. When the day is done, she unplugs her laptop, puts the cord away in its proper place, and slips the laptop into its designated spot in the bookcase, leaving only her phone on her desk before going home.

Even if you're working from home, it's important to grace your workplace with things that spark joy, rather than making it solely utilitarian. I like to keep a small plant and a shiny crystal on my desk. I choose memo pads that have a touch of playfulness and folders in my favourite colours. My main writing tool is one treasured pen, and I only keep the bare

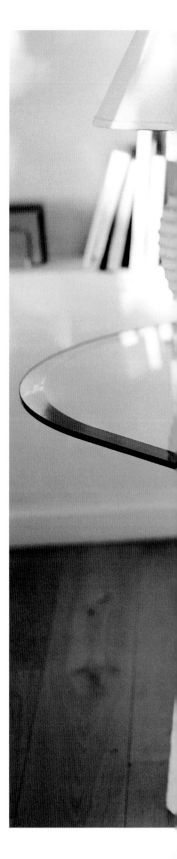

minimum of pencils and coloured pens, whose uses are identified by their shades. I use aromas such as mint or grapefruit to help me shift gears from task to task. If your home is your office, switching aromas is also a great way to switch from work mode to relaxing-at-home mode, and so is changing the type of music you play while on the job as opposed to during your personal time. If your dining or kitchen table doubles as your desk, I recommend putting your work-related items in a tray or basket and storing them out of sight once work is over, so you can relax without being reminded of tasks you still need to get done.

When I began offering tidying lessons in America, I was pleasantly surprised to find that Americans often decorate their desks or work spaces with personal things that bring them joy, such as photos of their family.

When we focus on ways to make our workspace a pleasure to work in, the space itself is bound to spark joy. The best place to start is by imagining your ideal way of working.

Take a moment to review how you want to start your day at work and what you spend time on, such as meetings, mulling over ideas, reading to gain inspiration, or gathering information. Then think about how to balance these activities in a way that would be pleasant for you and draw up a schedule based on that image. Assess the items in your workspace to see if they are helping you be productive and inspired. By taking time to reflect on our approach to work, we can bring our work life closer to our ideal.

Your bedroom is a base for recharging your energy for another day.

My ideal bedroom has a comfy bed with clean sheets and pillowcases and an atmosphere that invites me to give thanks for the day as I relax and fall asleep. The bedside lamp and the pictures on the walls are carefully chosen favourites. Gentle classical or relaxation music plays softly in the background, and the air carries a hint of lavender or rose. A vase with a single flower provides a soothing touch.

The first thing that one of my clients changed after tidying up was her bed linen. Until then she had been using blue sheets, but instead she began using pink ones that she found still in their package in the back of her closet. She felt the urge to wash them more frequently and discovered not only how pleasant it is to sleep on fresh sheets, but also that she really likes the colour pink.

'Before I go to sleep,' she told me, 'I now take a look around the room and mentally thank everything I see just for being there.'

One thing I avoid keeping in the bedroom are any items that give off unnatural light. If the light emitted by the green button on a lamp switch or burglar alarm is too bright, for example, I cover it up when I go to bed to keep the lighting conditions in my room as natural as possible.

Isn't it great to have a bedroom that helps you shed the fatigue of the day and recharges your energy?

And what if the first thing you saw in the morning was something that sparked joy? As we transition from sleep to wakefulness, our subconscious mind, which takes over during sleep, persists for a while alongside our conscious mind, which takes over during our waking hours. For this reason, I recommend arranging your room so the first things you see inspire positive thoughts and feelings.

If your window happens to look out on a beautiful landscape like the sea, that's wonderful. But even if your bedroom doesn't have a window, or your only view is the building next door, don't worry. Imagine what would give you the greatest pleasure if it was the first thing you saw when you woke up, and then design the interior of your room with that in mind. You can make a 'joy niche' in your bedroom simply by identifying the spot you'll look at first and placing something you love right there. It could be a vase of seasonal flowers, a house plant, or a work of art. You could place it on your bedside table or dresser, or, if there's no room, you could put up a wall display rack or hang a favourite picture or patterned cloth on the wall.

You don't need much. Design your bedroom with one focal point that inspires joy and makes waking up in the morning a pleasure.

What is your vision for a bedroom that inspires rest and gratitude? Where do you look when you first wake up, and what can you feature there to spark joy as soon as you open your eyes?

Organize your closet to uplift your spirits.

Engaging with your clothes in a mindful way will change your relationship with them and spark joy day in and day out. If your closet is overflowing and you dread opening the door, nothing will have a more immediate impact than folding your clothes. This simple act solves almost all clothing storage problems. Just switching from hanging to folding them creates more space.

So how do you determine whether to fold or hang an item? Anything flowy, like a billowy dress or skirt, should be hung. If you're not sure, place the item on a hanger and wave it in the air. If it dances merrily, it belongs on a hanger. Other things that should be hung are clothes with a lot of structure, like a coat or a suit jacket. Everything else can be folded.

Folding clothes is not merely the physical act of arranging cloth in a certain shape. Nor is it just about maximizing your storage space. When you run your hands over your clothes, you are communicating with them, imparting love and positive energy. The gentle pressure of your palms revitalizes the fibers. As you smooth out the fabric, thank your clothes for protecting you. Doing these things deepens your affection for each item in your wardrobe, reminding you of why they spark joy.

There's only one simple tip to folding clothes properly: fold each one into a smooth rectangle that stands upright. That's it. Every item will have its own favourite way of being folded. I call this the 'golden point'. Isn't it wonderful that you can spark joy each day simply by the way you fold your clothes?

Once you've finished folding and are ready to put them away, store each item vertically in a drawer so you can see where everything is at a glance. Make sure they fit snugly, and arrange them in a gradual colour gradient, keeping similar shades together. I arrange my drawers from light to dark, from the front of the drawer to the back. When you organize your clothes by colour, you can instantly tell how many of each you have.

Now it's time to organize your whole closet. The key is to create a line of clothes that rises to the right. When you open the door, just the sight of it will raise your spirits. Try drawing a rising line in the air with your fingertip. Can you feel how it gives you a lift?

To make this line, I hang long, thick, and dark-coloured items on the left and move toward short, light, and bright-coloured items so that the hemlines of the clothes curve upward to the right. It's best to organize them by type as well: coats with coats, dresses with dresses, and skirts with skirts. This makes the storage process very simple, and it's easy to find what you're looking for.

For shoes, if you have built-in closet shelves, you can dedicate a shelf or two to store them. If you don't, place a shoe rack under your hanging clothes. Regular shoes, like pumps and leather shoes, go on the bottom, while sandals and lighter shoes belong higher up. The same principles apply to shoe cupboards located by the entryway or mud room. It's best if people who are taller place their shoes higher up, while shorter people and children place theirs on the lower shelves.

If you have a walk-in closet with enough room on the walls, you can decorate the interior with items that bring you joy. Your closet is your own private space, so feel free to go all out and make it a special oasis or a distinctive tribute to your most quirky interests.

What do you want to see inside your closet to motivate and inspire you as you start your day?

Be Proud of Your Style Rut

To open your closet and see only clothes you love is exhilarating. Some people, however, are disappointed to find that, once they've gone through their entire wardrobe, the clothes remaining all seem alike – either similar in colour or the same style or brand.

One of my clients, whose final wardrobe was predominantly beige and green, confided to me that comments in fashion magazines lamenting style ruts always made her anxious. 'Because I wear the same type of outfit all the time too,' she explained. She had once branched out adventurously, purchasing clothes in red and blue. In the end, however, they never left her closet because she didn't feel comfortable wearing them.

'Perhaps they had fulfilled their purpose,' I suggested.

'But without these, my clothes will all be the same,' she protested. 'What if people at the office start calling me things like "the beige lady" or "the green Martian"?'

'Do you know anyone else who always wears the same type of clothes?' I asked her.

'Now that you mention it,' she said, 'I know quite a few.'

'When you see them, do you think it's strange and wonder why?'

'No,' she answered. 'In fact, I'd probably think it strange if they suddenly wore something different.'

That's right. Surprisingly, most of us don't notice when others wear similar outfits all the time. In fact, it's even reassuring and comforting to see them in the sort of clothes we've come to associate them with. I used to always wear the same type of clothes too: either a dress with a cardigan or blazer or a white top over a skirt. More than 80 per cent of my work outfits were probably one of these two combinations. It was only after I had children that my wardrobe diversified somewhat, because I began to wear more casual clothes. Most of my clients also end up with the same type of outfit once they've finished tidying their clothes. Even people whose wardrobe seems quite varied actually follow a characteristic pattern if you look closely at the colours or shapes they choose.

Tidying our clothes forces us to confront our past, including the mistakes we made as we learned what suits us. Our wardrobe will always contain some reminders of experiments we would rather forget. I'm embarrassed to think how many times I whispered to such items, 'Thank you for teaching me that this style isn't for me,' and then forced them as 'gifts' onto my younger sister, the recipient of my 'charitable donations' at one time in my life. (This, by the way, is an excellent example of what *not* to do.)

The clothes remaining at the end of this learning process, however, are definitely the ones that suit you best, the ones you feel most comfortable in. So, strut your fashion rut with confidence. It's the fashion industry that perpetuates the idea that we must always wear something different. Freeing ourselves from this misconception can be a huge relief and allow us to truly enjoy choosing what to wear.

But what if you long for a more colourful wardrobe? Once they've tidied their clothes, many of my clients go for colour assessments or attend fashion seminars to broaden their selection of clothes consciously and objectively. These are great ways to start branching out.

As for the beige-and-green client above, when she reached the stage of tidying her photos, which in the KonMari Method is the very last category, and began checking each one for joy, she suddenly burst out laughing. 'Look,' she said. 'Here's one from fifteen years ago.' The photo showed her in beige bottoms and a green top. 'Everyone in my family is dressed the same way they are now. My dad still wears gray pants and polo shirts, and my mom still wears a white T-shirt over a patterned skirt.' She smiled. 'That makes me feel much better. From now on, I'll proudly declare myself a green Martian.'

Although personally I think she didn't really need to call herself that, she carried on quite happily to complete her tidying festival.

Wiping the Soles of Your Shoes Brings Good Luck

Shoes have a strange appeal. While on the one hand they're consumables, on the other they're like accessories or even works of art. Some people's passion for shoes results in collections so vast they could not possibly wear them all. Even those who don't collect them have experienced love at first sight with at least one pair they bought on impulse.

I happen to love shoes myself – so much so that one day I sat down and gazed at mine intently. I took them all out of the cabinet, lined them up in the entranceway, knelt on the floor, and stared at them for about an hour. It's hard to explain why. I just had a sudden urge to listen to their troubles. They had shone so brilliantly in the shop, but now, shut away in the cabinet, they seemed to have lost their confidence.

'I know! I'll clean them,' I thought.

I took out my shoeshine kit and began polishing them one by one until they gleamed. When I was done and had laid them all out on a sheet of newspaper, I thought I heard them speak. 'Wipe our soles, too,' they seemed to say.

Open your shoe closet and take a look. Do you feel repulsed? Or captivated? The difference has nothing to do with the quality or price of your shoes.

During a lesson with one of my clients, I noticed something odd when we came to her shoes. She had gathered them all together and was picking them up one by one to ask if they sparked joy, but something seemed wrong. For one thing, they were laid out on crumpled sheets of old newspaper. And she held each one gingerly at arm's length, dangling it between her thumb and forefinger – even those shoes that looked like they might spark joy. I remembered her expression when I had asked her to take them all out. Hadn't she grimaced? Yes. She was treating her shoes as if they were disgusting, even though they had once been displayed like jewels in the shop.

No item in our wardrobe is treated as differently as our shoes before and after we purchase them. The reason, of course, is that once we start wearing them, they collect a lot of dirt. But that's because they spend all day confronting the dirt in our lives. Without a doubt, shoes have the hardest job of all.

Perhaps your shoes converse with their neighbours, your socks or stockings, while you are wearing them. 'It sure is hot today,' your shoes might say.

'Yes, positively steamy. Hang in there,' the socks might respond.

But privately, your shoes must be thinking, 'At least you get to freshen up by being washed every time you're worn.'

There's also a vast difference between the tops and the soles of our shoes. The tops are often kept well-polished, drawing admiring glances, whereas the soles are rarely so lucky. This seems heartless when it's the soles that take on the thankless job of tramping through the muck. They're the ones that should be given special treatment. We should really give them the respect they deserve.

That's why I adopted the habit of wiping the soles of my shoes before bed or first thing in the morning when I wipe down my entranceway. And as I do, I thank my shoes for supporting me all day.

Of course, sometimes I'm too busy, but when I can follow this routine, I find that it increases my clarity of mind more than cleaning anything else. I also feel like I can go places that suit clean shoes. There's a saying, 'Good shoes take you to good places', but it's really the soles of our shoes that get us there. After all, it's the soles that connect us to the ground.

If you make a habit of wiping the soles of your shoes, you may find that special things happen to you, like discovering a shop you really like or finding something you've always wanted when you stop by a store on a whim.

Only keep things in your bathroom that spark joy.

People tend to leave soap, sponges, and other utilitarian bath and cleaning items in plain view in the bathroom, but I recommend storing everything out of sight except the things you love to look at. For example, I keep cleansers and brushes in the cupboard, as well as shampoo and body wash if I think the package design won't bring me joy, only taking them out when I use them. Another option is to transfer your favourite shampoo and body wash into bottles you really like and put them on display. This way you can make sure your bathroom always sparks joy.

One of my clients in America tastefully arranged potted plants around their spacious bathroom so it felt like being in a garden. What a refreshing space to take a bath! While it would be lovely to have that much room, even with a small space you can create the effect you want by adding a few little plants.

Japanese homes, especially in the city, are generally much smaller than American homes, which means a large bathroom is usually out of the question. The one in the apartment I lived in was tiny, without much light, so I couldn't grow plants. Instead, whenever I had a bath, I took the single-flower vase that I kept in the living room and put it on a shelf to delight my eyes. I encourage you to make your bath time as special as possible by adding touches such as your favourite bath salts or candles.

How can you customize your bathroom storage or containers so they spark joy? What kinds of flowers or ornaments would you like to decorate your bathroom with?

Personalize Your Organizing Boxes and Drawers with Pops of Colour and Pattern

When you've finished tidying and have chosen those things that spark joy, it's time to redesign your storage to spark joy too. Personally, I prefer simple, beautiful containers made of wicker or bamboo or coloured black and white. I also like to use eco-friendly goods, such as cardboard boxes made from recycled paper or organic cotton cases.

If you're using clear plastic drawers, you can make them one of a kind by attaching beautiful postcards or wrapping paper to the front of the drawer on the inside. Drawers can spark joy when you open them too if you select dividers with that in mind. Think about how to divide the space to store everything upright so you can see where each item is at a glance.

It feels wonderful when you find just the right storage units to hold all the items that spark joy for you. Storage goods you already have on hand and even shoeboxes work great, but some people get a thrill from beautifully designed and sturdy containers bought specially for this purpose, and that's fine too.

It's fun to create your own ideal boxes and drawers – well organized with everything divided by category and in just the right amount.

Design your powder room to keep energy flowing.

When it comes to the powder room or water closet, cleanliness is everything. With so little storage space, regular cleaning is crucial. Although the amount of time you spend there is short, it's the 'detox area' of your house, and it's important that it doesn't feel clogged.

I recommend keeping your stock of toilet paper out of sight in a basket or under an attractive cloth. To purify the air, I personally prefer nonchemical air fresheners in wood fragrances, such as eucalyptus. In keeping with Japanese tradition, I place special slippers just inside my washroom door and choose a floor mat in matching tones. Other than that, all that is needed is a bit of decoration, such as a favourite postcard or ornament. Such items can be changed to match the season or your mood.

One of my clients decorated all four walls of her powder room from floor to ceiling with decals. The lower half of the walls was covered with long-stemmed poppies. She also laid a fluffy green mat that looked like grass on the floor. It was like stepping into another world and being immersed in a field full of flowers. This reminded me that we should feel free to experiment within our own home.

What would be the theme colour for your ideal powder room? What kind of fragrance in the powder room would make you happy?

Keep Your Home Healthy by Stimulating Its Pressure Points

Shiatsu, a Japanese form of acupressure, feels wonderful. My grandfather was an acupuncturist and moxibustion practitioner, as well as a scholar of traditional Chinese and Japanese medicine. Consequently, even as a child, I knew a lot about pressure points and how to stay healthy. My grandfather started giving me shiatsu and manipulative massage treatments when I was in elementary school, and as a high school student, I submitted myself quite willingly to acupuncture. He used an apparatus that looked like something from a dubious scientific experiment, sticking needles with wires attached into my pressure points and then running a mild electric current through them. 'Health is all about circulation,' he would say, beaming as he ruthlessly inserted another needle. Despite the way it looked, his method was very effective.

Having been raised in such an environment, words like *pressure point* and *circulation* have always been part of my life. So, when I'm tidying, it's quite natural for me to wonder where the home's pressure points are and what might be blocking the circulation of air. (If this sounds strange to you, feel free to dismiss it as an occupational disease that afflicts certain tidying professionals.)

But if there *were* pressure points in a house or apartment, where do you think they might be?

What places would let the air flow more freely if they were decluttered?

The answer is the entrance, the center, and any areas with plumbing. Although there are, in fact, many other pressure points, tackling these three produces the most dramatic results. I think it's fairly easy to see why clearing up areas with plumbing, such as the washroom and kitchen sink, is so effective. They are the first to show signs of use and therefore the most noticeable once tidied up. I've also explained how the entrance serves as a kind of shrine gate, cleansing us of all the dirt we bring home. What may be harder to grasp is the center.

The first time I visit a client, I always kneel formally and greet their home. I do this in the central spot. From the beginning, whenever I walked through a home, I would always sense a place where the air seemed to change, thickening and swirling like a whirlpool, and that spot would invariably be near the middle of the house. It didn't matter if it happened to be in a corridor or a storage room; the effect was always the same.

Sometime after I first made this discovery, I came across a diagram titled 'The Path of Energy Flow' in a book on feng shui. It showed that energy entering the front door circles in the center of the house and exits diagonally through the opposite wall. This was the same path of circulation I had sensed in my clients' homes. Once this central point is tidied up and kept uncluttered, air flowing in from the entrance will circulate much more freely, making the whole house feel lighter.

Now that you're aware of its existence, you can make this central home pressure point work for you in your daily life. You don't need to do anything special. And it doesn't matter if there's a pillar or a piece of furniture in this spot. Just keep it free of trash: make sure no one places a rubbish bin or items to be discarded there, or anything that has clearly served its purpose. Otherwise, a sense of unease will quickly pervade your entire home.

This reminds me of something my grandfather, a health fanatic who lived a long, full life, used to say: 'Keep your expression bright and your intestines light. Other than that, you just need to stay clean to be healthy.'

Applying this principle to our home, we should keep the entrance, or face, of our home bright; the center, or gut, free of clutter; and any areas with plumbing, like the bathroom and powder room, clean and shining. By paying attention to these three pressure points, we can keep our homes happy and healthy.

An organized garage is a joyful garage.

I used to think that a garage was just a place to park the car. When I moved to America I was astonished by their size. The average American garage is far larger than any I have ever seen in Japan. As a result, however, many people use them as storage space, and they are often packed with seasonal and miscellaneous items. Checking regularly on what you keep in your garage will help you keep tabs on how much stuff you actually have.

The way to transform your garage from a storage space into a joyful place is to tidy up. A central principle of the KonMari Method is to tidy by category, and it also applies to garages. I suggest breaking items down into such categories as decorations for special occasions, tools, camping gear, and so on. Just as when tidying your home, start by gathering every item in one category in the same spot, touching each one, and keeping only those that spark joy.

When you have finished choosing all the items that spark joy for you, store them by category. The key to storing items in a garage is to make it easy to see where everything is. This maximizes the garage's function as a storage space. If you can keep everything in containers of the same type, this will make the space look even neater. Dust and dirt infiltrate garages quite easily, so it's best to use containers with lids. Any items that can be placed vertically in the containers should be stored upright. The goal is to store everything in the container in such a way that you can see at a glance where each item is when you open the lid. If you label your containers and store them on wire racks, everyone in the family will be able to tell where things are kept.

To spark even more joy in your garage once you've completed the basic tidying process, I recommend decorating it with items you love, just as you would decorate your home. If there's an empty wall, use it to hang those pictures you didn't have room for inside the house, or make a special hobby corner. Decorating your garage transforms it from a parking spot or storage shed into a more joyful space. And thinking up ways to make it spark joy can be fun.

What kind of storage containers would you like in the garage? Plastic ones? Cardboard? Baskets? What kind of colour scheme and organizational system would work best? What kind of decorations would transform your garage?

Decorate Your Walls with the Scenery You Want to See

One day, in the middle of a tidying lesson, I found myself sitting in front of a mirror with a towel draped around my neck.

My client that day was makeup artist S. 'When it comes to makeup,' she said, 'balance is certainly important, but, in fact, the face is a collection of parts. There are some parts that you can change and others that you can't. You can't change your bone structure, for example. Just like you can't change the actual layout of your house by decorating it. And just as it's better to keep the floor free of clutter, the clearer your skin, the better.'

She opened her big makeup box, then continued with her lecture. 'Cheeks serve as supporting actors, but they can completely transform your face, depending on the colour of blush and how it's applied. A bit like indirect lighting, I suppose. Eyes are the windows that you frame. Extra layers of mascara function like gorgeous curtains.'

Throughout this explanation, she deftly applied makeup to my face. 'But if you want to change your image quite drastically and immediately, the best way is to change your hairstyle. Hair covers a lot of area and can be arranged in many ways, such as by putting it up or adding ornaments.'

She grasped my hair and demonstrated. 'So when you talk about how we need to decorate the walls, it's like dressing up your hair, don't you think?'

Right: walls. Now I remembered what had started all this. Half an hour ago I'd been talking about walls when she suddenly launched into this makeup lesson.

If you've finished tidying up but your home seems a little bare, the next step is to decorate your walls. Broadly defined, your home has four parts: floors, walls, windows, and doors. But, without a doubt, the most effective way to achieve an instant makeover is to focus on the walls. They cover a broad area and can be transformed at will with art, ornaments, or whatever you personally like.

I have about twenty framed pictures on the walls of my home, including some small ones in the powder room and entranceway. These include everything from proper oil paintings to casually framed pieces of embroidery, but they are favourites I've collected from the time I was single.

One, for example, is a print from Monet's *Water Lilies* series that I've had since I lived in an apartment in Tokyo. In that crowded city, I dreamed of living near the water, and I searched all over for a picture of the kind of scenery

I wanted to see from my window. When I stumbled upon Monet's water lilies floating on an emerald-green pond, it was love at first sight. Although it was just an inexpensive poster, I placed it in a window-sized frame. It now hangs in the powder room, on the opposite wall to the sink. That emerald pond still brings me joy each time I see it reflected in the mirror.

Some of my clients have also come up with interesting ideas. One who loves stargazing uses a home planetarium projector to cast a star-spangled sky across her wall at night. Another client, who has no window in the dining area, framed a poster of an English garden with a set of curtains, fulfilling her desire to gaze out on a flower garden while eating breakfast.

It seems like such a waste to leave our walls bare when we can use them to create the scenery we'd like to see from our room. What would you like to look out at?

If you've finished tidying up but things don't quite click, it's a sign you need to add some essence of joy. In that case, start by decorating your walls. Before you know it, you'll have a home that inspires delight.

Cultivate joy outdoors.

Ever since I was little, I dreamed of having a house with a garden. As a child, we lived in a condominium in the city, so all we had was a balcony. At that time, balconies in Japan functioned merely as places to hang the laundry. There was no space for plants. After I got married, we lived in an apartment that also had a balcony, but this time, I could use it for growing plants instead of hanging clothes, because we had a dryer. I covered the plain concrete floor with wooden pallets and lined up rows of planters and pots to create my own original garden. I can confidently say that it's possible to enjoy gardening with just a balcony.

When thinking about your outdoor space, it's important to imagine how you will spend time there. In my case, I wanted to sit on my balcony and admire my plants. I also wanted to be able to see them from the window. Modest aspirations, I know, but this dream was one I longed to fulfill.

If you live in a place that's not as well suited to growing things, such as a crowded city center or an arid region, you might want to spend time in your outdoor space differently. Maybe your ideal is to have an outdoor kitchen with a grill or fire pit, a space for meditation, or a mini putting range. Or perhaps you prefer to set a favourite chair outside where you can sip your morning coffee, put up a hammock for taking naps, make a play area for your kids, or have a table for gatherings of family and friends. Let your imagination run free as you conjure up images of the lifestyle that sparks joy for you.

If you have trouble imagining how you would like to spend time in your outdoor space, I suggest looking at different people's lifestyles, reading books about people who have integrated beautiful gardens into their lives, and examining attractive yards and decks in magazines or online. You are certain to find hints about how to use your own space. Just searching for the type of garden or outdoor environment that matches the lifestyle you want can spark joy.

Gardening Is Like Tidying

For the longest time, I thought I would never be any good at gardening. I love leafy house plants. When I was in Japan, I often tried growing some, but I had more failures than successes. I managed to wither a pachira I had placed in the entranceway, shriveled a favourite golden pothos plant, and wiped out all the herbs in my planter.

When I moved to America, I was surprised to learn it's quite common to hire a gardener. In our first home, which we rented, there was a lovely garden that was well-tended by a professional gardener. It was such a pleasure to spend time among the plants and watch them grow that an irresistible urge to try gardening bubbled up inside me. I began with a small herb garden, growing relatively popular plants, such as rosemary and lavender, which I could use in cooking. When I began to have success, I started thinking about what I wanted to try growing next, such as a flowering plant or vegetable, and gradually expanded the kinds of plants I raised.

I once helped tidy up an edible plant nursery as part of a project for a TV show. While there, I consulted the people who worked in the nursery about my own garden and asked them to describe how they approached their work. They told me the secret of success is to 'just try it' and encouraged me to experiment with whatever appealed to me. They also told me that to make my own dream garden, all I needed was a little basic knowledge about things such as how to mix fertilizer into the soil and the best time to plant specific varieties. Their encouragement and advice further fueled my passion for gardening.

'Just try it' and 'Do it with tender, loving care'. These words apply to tidying as well as to gardening. How many people put off gardening for years, telling themselves they'll do it someday, also reminds me of tidying up. Imagine your ideal garden, design it to spark joy, and plant things that make you happy. Remember to use tools that delight you as well. Look for a trowel with a cute design or a pot that speaks to you. As you gradually collect tools that spark joy, you will derive more pleasure from gardening. Again, these are the same principles that increase our joy in tidying and also in our daily lives.

CHAPTER 4

Your Joyful Morning

Having a great day depends on how we wake up and get going. This chapter will help you think through your ideal morning so you can focus on the practices and behaviours that spark joy.

What kind of morning would boost your joy factor all day long?

For me, the best way to start my day is to open the window and let in some fresh air. When we wake in the morning, I think we're a completely different person from who we were the day before. Sleep has dispelled any pent-up frustrations, and we feel brand new. So, the first thing I want to do is let the fresh air cleanse my space of any lingering fogginess.

I light some incense, choosing fragrances such as frankincense, lavender, or palo santo, depending on my mood. In many places, incense smoke is used to symbolically purify a space, which is why it's burned during Buddhist ceremonies to drive away misfortune. Once I feel refreshed, I say, 'Good morning!' to my house just like I would greet my family – a custom I started when I began living on my own.

To refresh my body, every morning I rinse out my mouth and gargle. I recently began using Ayurvedic oil as a rinse, a custom known as oil pulling. Once my mouth feels clean, I drink a cup of hot water. This helps clear my stomach before I eat breakfast. Whenever possible, I wait until I feel hungry before eating, doing some housework or finishing up a work-related task first so my gut begins working. I find that eating breakfast after I've cleaned out my system really boosts my metabolism, making me feel lighter and more energetic.

It Takes Just Ten Days of Effort to Develop New Habits

What habits should we acquire to make each day more joyful?

Burning incense, exercising, emptying out my bag when I get home – these are just some of the daily habits I have developed. On the surface, acquiring a new habit seems like a lot of trouble, so some people give up before they even try, deciding it's impossible or that they're too busy. It's difficult to form new habits. But for me, there is one key approach that seems to work: try it every day for ten days. Just like the KonMari principle of tidying, do it thoroughly and completely, in a short period of time.

Why won't it work to do it every three days instead of daily? Because it's the first step, the period when we begin to change a pattern of behaviour, that requires the most energy.

First, it's far easier to motivate yourself and stick with something if you set an initial goal of just ten days instead of telling yourself to do something daily forever from now on. Second, if you start by developing a habit of doing something every three days, you'll then have to exert more energy to start doing it daily. Dividing the process into two stages is simply a waste of effort.

Although at first it may seem like a lot of work, it's only ten days. If you practise your new habit for that limited period, it will be easier to develop a rhythm. Pretty soon you'll start to savour the pleasure this habit brings: perhaps it's one that clears your mind, makes something easier, helps you find a place to keep every item you own, or lets you reset yourself at the end of the day.

I adopted the habit of Ayurvedic oil pulling only recently, rinsing my mouth every morning with white sesame oil. In the beginning, the taste made me gag, and I wondered if it was really as good as I had heard. After doing it continuously for ten days, however, my skin became more supple, and I got used to the way the oil felt inside my mouth. I've kept it up without interruption ever since.

Of course, if you realize during those ten days that you can't make it a daily habit or that you'll enjoy it more if you do it just once every four days, you can readjust your routine accordingly. If you're going to start something new, I think it's easier to set the hurdle high to begin with and experience the ultimate joy your new habit can bring.

This approach works best for things that don't require any skill, such as emptying your bag every night. Whereas it takes years of practice to learn a new language or the piano, if you pick something anyone can do, you can experience the effects almost immediately.

So starting today, for the next ten days, what new habit would you like to develop? If you've already completed your tidying festival, I'm sure you can successfully create any new habit you choose.

Take time to fuel your good health with breakfast.

Breakfast in our house is usually Japanese style. We always have rice, which we cook in a traditional earthenware pot known as a donabe, and miso soup, plus eggs or leftovers from the previous night's dinner. This makes for a simple but highly nutritious breakfast. While waiting for the rice to cook, I check my schedule and look over the tasks I need to do that day.

The atmosphere surrounding the morning meal is just as important as the menu. We do our best to make sure our whole family eats together before our children go off to school, often playing soothing music, such as classical piano, in the background. This helps them leave home feeling happy.

If you usually eat breakfast at home, I recommend adding a few touches to make this time special. When we allow our phones to distract us during the meal, or just snatch a few bites of whatever happens to be there as we grab our keys and head out the door, we lose the opportunity to make breakfast a precious part of our day, and that seems a waste.

Still, there are times when I'm so busy, the whole aim of breakfast is just to get food into everyone's stomach, and I start nagging my children to hurry up and eat. During moments like these, I pause to reflect, then strive to make breakfast as positive an experience as possible.

Marie's miso soup

SERVES 4

720ml water

1 (10cm) piece kombu

2 dried shiitake mushrooms

250g cubed tofu (firm or soft, based on your preference)

30g fresh spinach, chopped

1 tablespoon dried wakame (optional)

2 tablespoons homemade miso (see recipe page 126), or shop-bought miso paste

We have miso soup for breakfast every day. It's simple to make; all you need is dashi soup stock, miso, and some veggies or other ingredients. I make my own miso paste and soup stock from scratch as often as possible, but using shop-bought miso and stock results in a delicious soup too. Making your own miso paste is also easy (see my recipe for a homemade version on page 126). You just mash cooked soya beans, add salt and koji (malted rice), and mix well. Place the mixture in an airtight container and let it ferment. It will be ready to use in about 6 months. And it keeps well, so if I make 4 kilograms at a time, I only need to make a batch once or twice a year.

For an easy and delicious dashi soup stock, soak a strip of kombu (dried kelp) and a couple of dried shiitake mushrooms overnight. If you're pressed for time, see the variation below to make a quick stock.

Feel free to customize your miso soup additions – I like to add tofu, spinach, and wakame, but you can toss in whatever sparks joy for you.

Pour the water into a medium-sized pot, add the kombu and dried shiitake, and soak overnight.

When you're ready to make the soup, place the pot over medium heat. Just before the water comes to a boil, turn off the heat and use a slotted spoon to remove the kombu and shiitake. Finely slice the kombu and shiitake and return them to the pot or reserve them for another use.

CONTINUED

MARIE'S MISO SOUP, CONTINUED

Add the tofu, spinach, and wakame and bring the stock to a boil over medium heat. Remove the pan from the heat.

Place the miso in a small bowl. Using a ladle, slowly add stock to the bowl and stir until the miso is completely dissolved. Pour the miso into the pot and stir it into the stock.

Return the pot to low heat and bring the soup almost to a simmer. Immediately remove the pot from the heat and ladle the soup into bowls to serve. The soup is best on the day it is made.

Variation: To make a quick stock, replace the kombu and shiitake mushrooms with 1 teaspoon instant dashi powder or bonito soup stock. Bring the water to a boil over high heat. Turn the heat to low, add the powder, and stir until dissolved. Continue the recipe as directed.

Miso

MAKES 3.6 KILOGRAMS

900g dried soya beans (organic, if possible)

900g dried rice koji

450g salt, plus more for sprinkling and weighting

Place the soya beans in a large pot with a lid and add lukewarm water to cover. Swish the soya beans around and then drain them in a colander. Repeat this process two or three times until the water is clear and there's no foam on the surface. Place the rinsed soya beans back into the pot and add enough water to cover the beans by about 7.5cm. Soak the beans overnight or for at least 10 hours.

Drain the soaked beans and return them to the pot with enough water to cover. Bring to a boil over high heat, then reduce the heat to low and simmer, with the pot partially covered to allow steam to escape, for 2 to 3 hours, until the beans are soft enough to crush between your thumb and pinky finger. Stir occasionally to keep the beans from sticking to the bottom of the pot and add more water as needed to keep the beans submerged.

Drain the beans, reserving the cooking water. Using a potato masher, mash the warm beans, skins and all, until smooth. Alternatively, you could place the beans in a sturdy plastic bag and use a rolling pin or the palm of your hand to mash them. Note: warm beans are easier to mash than beans that have cooled, so work fast. After mashing, let the beans cool to at least 30°C before adding the koji.

In a large bowl, combine the koji and salt. Add the mashed and cooled soya beans and mix thoroughly with a large spoon. Using your hands, form the mixture into firmly packed balls about the size of a baseball (7.5cm in diameter). If the mixture is too dry to form into balls, add a little of the soybean cooking water until it holds together. Press the balls firmly and tightly, one at a time, into a large airtight container with a lid. Mould the miso to the shape of the container so no air pockets remain between the balls of miso or between the miso and the container. Ensure the top surface of the miso is flat and smooth.

Sprinkle the surface lightly and evenly with salt and press a piece of plastic wrap or parchment paper tightly over the surface to ensure no air remains between the miso and the plastic. Place a 2kg bag of salt on top of the plastic to weigh it down and place the lid on the container.

Store in a cool, dark place, such as a pantry or drawer, for at least 6 months before opening. After fermentation is complete, the miso can be stored in an airtight container in the refrigerator for up to a year.

Family mornings are like conducting a symphony.

The key to a joyful morning is not to feel too rushed. I think it's important to allow yourself a little extra time. My husband gets up around 4:00, so by the time I wake up at 6:00, he has already gotten a fair bit of work done. I wake the children at 6:30 so they can start getting ready for school. Then we all sit down to a leisurely breakfast before the children leave. That's my family's idea of how to spend a joyful morning.

The key to making extra time is to always return everything you need in the morning to its designated spot, one that has been chosen for ease of use. The children, for example, will need such things as their hairbrushes, school bags, and water bottles to get ready for school. We keep these in clearly designated spots so that everything goes smoothly when they wake up, with no time wasted rushing around looking for things.

To ensure our children can get up in time, we make certain they go to bed early enough. Before bed, they choose the clothes they will wear the next day. This cuts down on the time they need to get ready in the morning. If they sleep in and it looks like we won't have as much time, we switch the menu to easy-to-eat finger foods, such as rice balls stuffed with something nutritious. That way we don't have to nag our children to hurry.

Whether you have children or not, the approach is the same. Consider what you can do in the evening to avoid a big rush in the morning, and then prepare in advance to make everything go as smoothly as possible. With time to spare, your morning will be sure to spark joy.

Why not give yourself the gift of a lovely morning complete with your favourite music?

Put thought into customizing your morning.

In this chapter, I describe what I consider to be an ideal morning now that my family and I live in America. The content has changed somewhat, along with my lifestyle, as I have transitioned from being a single working person to being married and then to being a parent. The basic flow of time, however, remains essentially the same.

Of course, I wasn't able to achieve my ideal right from the start. To be honest, my mornings were often such a mad rush when I was single that I couldn't even remember what I had done. And if I slept in, the whole morning was shot.

One day, however, I sat down and seriously considered what my ideal morning would look like.

I opened my notebook and wrote down how I would like to spend my morning, including a time schedule and a photo of a delicious-looking breakfast taken from a magazine. Every so often I would look at this page, until gradually I almost forgot it existed. Then one day, I realized my mornings had become just like my ideal.

Based on personal experience, I believe that creating moments of joy between the time we get up and the time we leave the house or start work can dramatically increase our joy factor for the rest of the day.

Of course, not everyone's ideal is to get ready to leave home at such a leisurely pace. One of my clients told me her ideal is to leave the house within ten minutes of getting up and enjoy some time away from home before work. She gets everything ready the night before, takes ten minutes to shower, dress, and put on her makeup, then goes out for breakfast in a café. You might think achieving your ideal morning is an impossible dream, but once you've finished putting your house in order, it often happens quite naturally.

So how would you like to start your day? What kind of morning would boost your personal joy factor all day long?

Use as Few Cleansers as Possible

When I was a student, I went through a phase where I was really into cleaning our home whenever my mother was out. This wasn't because I wanted to do something nice for her, but rather because I couldn't suppress my compulsion to tidy. Not content with tidying my own room, I cleaned as a way to distract myself from tidying everyone else's rooms. I used bleach to clean the kitchen sink drain, scrubbed the grime from the kitchen fan, wiped the windowsills, and took great pleasure in removing dust that no one had even noticed, using different types of cleansers to tackle each type of dirt.

Now, however, there are almost no cleansers in my home at all. I have one each for the kitchen, the laundry area, and the toilet, plus a bag of baking soda. I use nothing whatsoever for the bathtub. Instead, after I've drained it, I wash it down with cold water from the shower to cool it, and then wipe it dry with a towel designated for this purpose. Spraying the tub with cold water is something I learned from my mother, but I decided to stop using cleansers because I find the chemical smell unpleasant. Not using cleansers seems to make no difference at all. I do, however, talk to the bath as I wipe it dry, saying things like, 'That was such a refreshing bath,' and 'It's amazing how you're always so clean and free from mould.'

I used to wipe the floor with cleanser as well, but now I just wipe it with a damp rag. I use ordinary white cotton ones. They don't stay white for long, and the sight of them doesn't spark joy, but I ignore that. I wash and dry them thoroughly, fold them using the same principles as those for folding clothes, and store them in their own box in a way that does bring me joy. When they become too grungy, I use them to wipe down things like the window and door screens before throwing them away.

I don't use cleanser for the stovetop either, but merely wipe it with a hot, damp cloth. This is something I learned from one of my clients. It's easy to remove oil and grease if you wipe the stovetop immediately after cooking using a well-wrung cloth soaked in hot or cold water.

I think that one of the keys to easy cleaning is to use the bare minimum of cleaning equipment. Of course, some people, such as professional cleaners, may need to use an array of cleansers to meet specific needs, while others may need to use them occasionally, such as to remove grime that has become firmly fixed. And if you are someone who actually enjoys collecting and trying out different kinds of cleansers, that joy itself is wonderful.

In my case, however, what brings me joy is a simple approach that requires just one cleanser so I don't have to think or choose. Fortunately for me, all-purpose cleansers that are good for the environment are now easy to find.

If, when you go through your cleansers, you find that you don't use some of them, why not take the opportunity to let them go and experiment with a simpler approach? The sight of a tidy cupboard, no longer filled with a jumble of cleansers, may actually inspire you to clean. Before you know it, your dream of a sparkling, joy-filled home will have come true.

CHAPTER 5

Your Joyful Day

To get the most joy out of your day, think about all the ways you spend your time, from the errands you run to the people you interact with. By learning to identify what's sparking joy for you in your daily life and what's just wasting precious energy, you can tidy up your routine and enjoy the life-changing results.

Cherry-pick your activities and routines.

Do you ever find your daily life is busier than you want it to be? Do you feel exhausted or have too many things to do?

Sometimes this happens to me. When it does, I take stock of how I'm using my time. I look through my diary and make a list of all the things I normally do. Then I assess whether I'm wasting time on irrelevant things, and if there are any items I can weed out.

Listing all our daily activities, including things like work, meetings, chores, miscellaneous tasks, hobbies, recreation, lessons, exercise, and time spent with family and friends, helps us identify which ways of spending our time bring us joy. Through this self-reflection, we may also discover that we've developed needless habits, such as scrolling through random news stories online, getting sucked into shopping sites while searching for something else, or popping into the kitchen for a snack every time we pass it.

Writing down how I spend my time helps me identify areas where I'm wasting it. It also helps me think about how I might make more efficient use of it, such as by changing the way I approach household chores or the order in which I prepare a meal. I always make sure to check whether I'm setting aside time to relax and take a break. Giving myself time to zone out makes me more efficient when I tackle other things.

Sometimes I reflect on my own, but I also reflect with my husband. This helps me recognize habits I tend to overlook. If I notice a bad habit, such as tending to overeat snacks when my family is around, I'll announce it. The next time my hand mindlessly reaches for a snack when I'm with them, I'm more likely to catch myself before I start munching. This is why I recommend telling your family what habits you want to quit – you're more likely to notice them and stop yourself.

Writing everything down or consulting someone about the way we use our time can help us be more aware of the shocking amount of time we waste.

After reviewing her schedule, one of my clients realized she wanted to spend more time with her family. She consciously increased her communications with family members and planned visits to those who lived far away. Changing the way she used her time brought her closer to her family, deepening her familial bonds.

Take a look at each activity you do. Is it worth scheduling into your life? Or would you rather reorganize your day to spend time on something more precious?

Let's tidy up the way we use our time each day so we can devote our lives to things that fill us with joy.

Create a harmonious family schedule.

Raising children can be quite challenging for parents. If you're a parent, believe me, I can relate. One never-ending issue is how to balance work and child-rearing, while another is how to create a support system with your family and the others around you.

In our case, one important way for my husband and I to create a harmonious family schedule is to make sure we each get a block of time alone to concentrate on what we need to get done. Many elements of our children's schedules can't be changed, so we start by aligning our schedules with theirs. Going to bed at the same time as the children and waking up at 4:00 in the morning to work seems to suit my husband's rhythm best. I, on the other hand, like to get my most important tasks done while the children are out. We adjust our work schedules so that one of us can be there for the children when they come home. Of course, when we're both out on business, we arrange for someone else to pick the children up from school and take care of them until we get back.

Each person's rhythm is different. Some find it easier to make time early in the morning. Others are at their best at night. What's important is for parents to consult with each other and ensure that they can schedule some personal time during the day when it's easiest for them to focus. Instead of assuming that having children means we can never have a moment to ourselves, we need to change our mindset and relish the challenge of scheduling this time into our day.

Teach your children to tidy as part of playtime.

In our family, we include chores and tidying as part of playtime. Before, I used to try and finish all the housework while the children were at school, but I ended up not getting any work done, and then I had to work after the children came home. One day, however, it hit me that I should just do the housework with them.

When I'm sewing on a button, my children want to try it too, so I let them sew one on the jacket of a stuffed toy. When I'm folding clothes, I announce, 'Time to fold', and they'll join right in. Afterward, we might decide it's snack time.

We also integrate tidying into playtime. If the children decide they want to draw when they're in the middle of playing with their blocks, I'll say, 'But we need to put these away first, right?' Tidying as they go along has become a natural part of their play. After playing, they're allowed to watch TV. Knowing they have to tidy up first, they work quickly to put everything away. Tidying is easy because all their toys have a fixed place and just need to be put back where they belong.

For our children, tidying has simply become a normal part of the day rather than something they *have to* do even though they hate it. I think this is because ever since they were toddlers, we've made it a habit to tidy up after each toy or activity before going on to the next.

If the children seem to be accumulating too many toys, we donate some of them. As we always decide where to keep each new toy we get, it's been clear to our children from the start that we only have a limited

amount of storage space. 'We bought this new toy', I'll say, 'but look, there's no place to put it. We'll have to give up one of the older toys, one that you don't play with any more, to make room.' Then I'll suggest giving it to someone who will play with it more or ask them if it might make the toy happy to become a present.

If you want to store any toys or baby clothes for your next child, decide where you're going to keep them. When tidying, it's important to face the fact that the size of your house and your storage space is limited. Whatever you decide to keep reduces the amount of living space you have. In our house, for example, we have set aside space for two containers of clothes we're saving for the next child. Once we know how much storage space we have, we can see more clearly which things we should keep.

Store Toys Intentionally

When I tidy up toys, I use a combination of bins for larger items and baskets and boxes for smaller items. I store everything upright, like with like. This lets me see where things belong, and how much we own, and makes it easy for our children to tidy up by themselves.

For storing smaller things, I recommend boxes. These can be used in two ways. One is the conventional way: as a container with a closed lid to keep a set of items together. Another is to use the lids as trays or dividers and the boxes as containers. For example, you can use a deep box to hold taller items like markers, glitter, glue, or paint, and then use the lid to store smaller items like rubber stamps or magnets. Semi-transparent pouches with zippers are perfect for keeping things like stickers and origami flat and can be placed upright in a basket. You can even use larger pouches to hold board game pieces, eliminating the need to store their bulky boxes.

Display the toys that spark the most joy on a low shelf that your children can reach. This curated collection will encourage play, and the toys can be swapped out from time to time to keep things fresh and exciting.

Keep your work life tidy.

In my experience, being a workaholic at some point in your life isn't always a bad thing. When I was around 20, I gave three tidying lessons a day. Each lesson took five hours, which meant I worked from 6:00 in the morning until 11:00 at night. But I was young and wanted to devote this period to working.

Finding a comfortable balance between work and private life will not only differ from one person to another, but will also depend on what stage of life each person is in. What's important is to take a good look at what kind of working style you want right now and what kind of balance between your job and private life seems right for you.

For example, if a particular project is one of the most important ones you'll ever work on in your career and you don't care if only 20 per cent of your time is left for private pursuits, then it's fine to arrange your schedule and that stage of your life to give your work priority.

What we should avoid is working flat-out while feeling frustrated or confused about whether this is really what we should be doing. When we work without a sense of purpose or direction and get swept along with the flow, we end up feeling pressured. That's the time to take a break and reflect on our lifestyle.

After I began balancing my career with child-rearing, I could no longer work the way I had when I was single. Although I was used to working long hours, I had no choice but to give that up. But having only a limited amount of time can help us find ways to use that resource more

effectively. Just as limited storage space makes it easier to decide what to keep and where, time constraints actually made it easier for me to organize my time.

How much time do you spend a day on each work-related task? How much work do you get done in a week? How do you balance your time to accomplish that? Which part of your job brings you the most joy? Are there any tasks you do out of habit that you could do without? Are there any you could do more efficiently? Are there some meetings you could eliminate? Are there steps you could take to increase time for relaxation? Take a moment to reflect on your daily work in this way.

For a joyful work life, find the balance that feels right for you.

Revel in creative outlets.

Let me get a little philosophical here. What do you see as the purpose of your life?

Ultimately, I think the purpose of life is to be happy and fulfilled. I don't mean this in a selfish, 'me first' way. When we exude an aura of happiness, this positive energy spreads to those around us, making the whole world a better place. To meet that larger goal, I think we each need to find happiness in harmony with those around us. So, what do we need in our daily lives to make this possible? I think one element is discovering our creative outlets and reveling in them.

Looking back on things we've always wanted to try or that we enjoyed as a child can provide insights into what creative activities we find fulfilling. For example, after my children were born, I loved spending time with them on things like sewing and knitting. This reminded me of all the things I'd enjoyed doing as a child – even tidying. It was only after tidying became my profession that I realized I'd enjoyed it since childhood.

Taking time to reflect on things like this can help us rediscover our own inner joy. It's common to forget what we loved as a child by the time we grow up. But when we stop and look at the things we naturally gravitate toward, we'll find that they're linked to what gives us joy.

I recommend asking yourself what creative outlets bring you joy, and then increasing the time you spend reveling in those activities. Tapping into your creativity, such as learning an instrument or painting, is a great way to experience more joy every day.

Store Komono Purposefully

Although komono can be found in almost every home, the number of categories is overwhelming, which is why they generate the majority of questions from my clients. By far the most common question, however, is: 'How can I possibly store them in a way that sparks joy when I have so many?'

The basic principle of storage is to store by category, so the first step is to break komono down into categories such as stationery supplies, electrical cords, medicines, and tools. Once that's done, I recommend storing categories that seem similar near each other. For example, you could store electrical cords near your computer or camera, because all of these are electrical in nature. Or, like some of my clients, you could store komono that fall into a daily-use category near your computer, such as stationery goods, and then identify each successive category as if it were a word-association game. Although categories for komono seem clearly defined on the surface, they often overlap a little, merging like gradations of colour, so as you store similar categories side by side, imagine yourself creating a beautiful rainbow in your house.

One of the most enjoyable parts of the tidying process can be planning storage for hobby-related komono, such as sewing items, paints and paintbrushes, or sticker collections.

These items themselves bring us joy, so focus on ways to make even opening the boxes in which they're stored a delight. For this, I recommend using special storage goods such as cute, antique-style boxes or carefully selected containers. I tend to be very particular, so at the moment I don't have many hobby containers. But it's fine to spend more time on this because the process of choosing what you want for your hobbies and interests, as well as the containers you want to store them in, is such a pleasure.

Recently, I've taken up embroidering with our children. I found a lovely pair of antique scissors that makes this even more fun. I love to browse through different antique shops to choose things like that, but when I don't have time, I look online. I'm sure those of you who love making handicrafts can understand how much joy the time spent searching brings me.

You may be worried that you've accumulated too many hobby-related items, but I'm all for that. There's no need to discard things that bring you joy. Even if it takes more time, I encourage you to store them in ways that make you happy.

157

Movement helps your energy flow.

Every morning, after sending our children off to school, tidying up the kitchen, and putting in a load of laundry, my husband and I set out for a walk. We use this time to check in with each other. Our walk often serves as a work meeting as well.

I've found that by integrating exercise into my routine in this enjoyable and productive way, I'm more likely to keep it up.

If you find yourself thinking you hate exercising, dig a little deeper. Are there any movements that spark joy for you? Some people love to dance, and some are inspired by hiking in nature. Others (like me) prefer to center themselves with yoga in the mornings or evenings or even get daily exercise by cleaning or vacuuming.

What movements spark joy for you? How can you turn them into a daily practice to get energy flowing through your body? These joyful movements can become your personal source of vitality.

Cleaning the Floor Is a Time for Meditation

In Japan, it's customary for elementary school children to clean their own classrooms and school corridors. One job is wiping the floors. They push all the desks and chairs against the wall and grab a damp rag. Positioning themselves in what resembles the Downward Dog yoga pose, with knees slightly bent and arms and back straight, they push the rag ahead of them as they scuttle up and down the length of the room, until the whole floor is done. By the time they finish, the floor is shining. Having been raised in this culture, I always wipe the floor in this way after vacuuming.

In a book on the Oriental treatment called seitai, which combines acupressure with chiropractic massage, I once read that the Japanese style of wiping the floor is ideal for straightening out kinks in the body and restoring balance. This makes sense to me, because after about five minutes of doing it, my breathing becomes smoother, my back straightens out, and I feel much better overall. When our body is properly aligned, we feel refreshed right to our emotional and mental center, solutions come to us more easily, and little worries no longer bother us. In that sense, wiping the floor is like practicing yoga or meditation while doing housework.

Another thing I noticed when I began cleaning my floors this way is that it became a form of dialogue with my home. The floor is the foundation of the house. Cleaning it with my own hands helps me to feel my connection to it, and that makes me appreciate it even more. When I focus my thoughts on how grateful I am for the support my house gives me all day long, it seems to respond, and the polished flooring feels warmer.

Of course, hiring professional cleaners or using a mop to clean the floors, especially in a large house, helps us use our time more efficiently. Since I began living in America, I've been hiring professional cleaners as well. But I actually like cleaning the floors, so sometimes I still get down and polish the floor as a form of enjoyable exercise.

According to the philosophy of feng shui, cleaning the floor, the home's foundation, attracts good news and increases one's financial luck. If you've been feeling irritable or have less opportunity to get out and exercise than before, why not try wiping the floor? It's good for both your mind and body, as well as for your house. And who knows – it may even increase your good fortune.

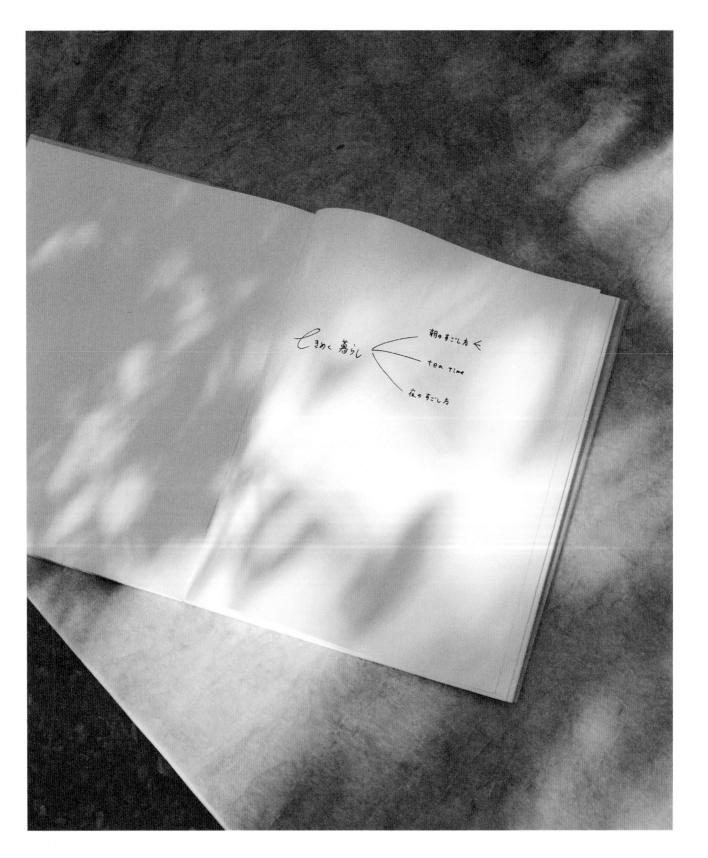

Take a moment for teatime.

I always make sure to take a tea break three times a day: once in the morning after sending the children off to school, once in the afternoon as a break from work, and once before bed. During teatime, I avoid looking at my phone or laptop. Instead, I sit on the sofa and relax while listening to classical music.

Working for long hours at a stretch reduces our efficiency. When we're physically and mentally tired, it's easy for our minds to get caught in a rut and go round and round the same thought. Taking time out from work to enjoy a nice cup of something is a great way to snap out of that mode.

So right from the start, schedule breaks into your day. Even just ten or fifteen minutes makes a difference. Of course, you may prefer to take a different type of break. Consider what you find most refreshing. A walk around the block? A short meditation? An afternoon espresso?

Since tea is what sparks joy for me, I make sure to have many different kinds on hand, including black tea, matcha, Chinese tea, and herbal teas. I choose the kind that most suits my mood on a given day.

Matcha latte

SERVES 1

Matcha, traditional powdered green tea, is now popular around the world. When I drink matcha, I like to prepare it with a little ceremony, complete with a traditional bamboo measuring spoon and bamboo whisk. Every movement – from measuring the tea to whisking and drinking it – is very relaxing, like a meditation, which makes teatime extra special. A recent favourite in our house is a matcha espresso machine that grinds the tea into a powder and turns it into a delicious matcha latte. But as you will see below, you don't need any fancy equipment to make your own matcha latte at home.

Heat the water to 80°C, or just simmering. Using a fine-mesh sieve, sift the matcha powder into a mug. Add the hot water and whisk the matcha and water until well combined and foamy. Heat and foam the milk using the steam wand of an espresso machine, an electric milk frother, or a handheld frother. Pour the frothed milk into the mug and whisk again. Add sweetener to taste and enjoy immediately.

60ml water

1 tablespoon matcha powder

240ml milk of your choice

Sweetener of your choice

Treasure the relationships and social activities that spark joy in your heart.

Do the relationships in your life bring you joy?

If we want our lives to spark joy, then we need to think about our relationships with our family, as well as those with our coworkers, friends, neighbours, and fellow members of different groups. Take time to reflect on each one.

If you feel that a certain relationship lacks joy, I recommend examining possible causes and reflecting honestly on your own feelings. Perhaps you'll notice something that caused a strain between you or realize that personality differences make it hard for you to get along. In such cases, it can help to think of concrete strategies for calming your mind when you're with them. For example, you could make a point of always greeting that person whenever you pass them. Or if there's no way to get along, you may decide it's better to withdraw from the relationship. As you readjust your relationships in this way, it's important to focus on building ones that spark joy.

For me, another important point is to pay attention to those who make a difference in my life and really appreciate them. Someone once told me that they write down the names of everyone they feel grateful for. This seemed like such a lovely idea that I adopted it myself. I highly recommend it. Write their names in a notebook while recalling what they do for you and the different ways they support you. As you remind yourself of how much you appreciate them, you'll become aware of how precious your relationship with them is and will naturally begin treating them with greater kindness, thanking and contacting them more often. This will make your relationships much easier.

Giving back to your community fosters gratitude.

Contributing to the community seems to be an integral part of American culture, an attitude I've come to appreciate more deeply since moving to the States. When I helped a community to tidy up their church, for example, it was clear from the way everyone pitched in that they supported one another regularly as a neighbourhood, and I was reminded of the importance of this very natural act.

I no longer live in Japan, but I still think about how I can give back to my home country. One way is to share Japan's wonderful artisanship and culture. A big part of that is, of course, introducing the KonMari Method, which grew from my Japanese cultural roots. But I can share other things as well. Take, for example, finely crafted traditional donabe earthenware cooking pots and bento boxes. Rather than just using these in my own personal life, I can introduce them to a wider audience through my online shop. Or I can take my favourite Japanese organic cotton and collaborate with designers to produce things like garment bags and dish towels. I can also share traditional Japanese cultural practices such as flower arrangement, the tea ceremony, and the custom of leaving our outdoor shoes at the entryway. Even if I no longer live in Japan, I can still contribute. The thought that I can give back to the place where I was born and raised gives me joy.

When considering how you can give back to society, a good place to start is to think about the kind of community you belong to and ask yourself what kinds of things you could do within that community. What can you contribute? How can you help? Are there organizations you

can donate to? Even if you can't find a concrete action to take at the moment, consider how you can express your gratitude to those who are contributing right now. What can you do to make others in your community happier? Can you introduce a new approach or technology that would help things run more smoothly or suggest eliminating an outdated approach that no longer serves the community's needs?

Think of ways to contribute to society that will make every day spark joy – not only for you, but also for those around you.

CHAPTER 6

Your Joyful Evening

To make sure your evenings spark joy, let's take a look at how you spend your time from dinner until you go to bed. How would you like to end your day?

Favourite family recipes spark connection and promote health.

If you live with your family and want to make suppertime spark joy, start by thinking about how you can all sit down together. If you live alone, think about ways to add joy to your surroundings, such as choosing a favourite tablecloth or place mat, arranging your table setting in your own special style, using decorative chopstick holders, or placing a vase of flowers on the table. Connecting with family or with yourself at the end of a busy day is precious. When eating with others, it's nice to share what brightened up each person's day.

Like breakfast, dinner at our house is almost always Japanese style. To make sure our family eats healthy meals that bring them joy, we plan menus that include fermented foods and provide a good balance of vegetables and proteins. Our children are still small, but they love my spinach with sesame sauce. Another dish they love is black vinegar chicken wings, a recipe passed down from my mother.

If you have recipes from your parents or grandparents that are just jotted on pieces of notepaper or recipe cards, why not take the opportunity to make them sparkle? Find and decorate a folder or box you love, or design your own container. This will not only keep your recipes together but will also store them in a way that continues to bring you joy.

If all your recipes are in cookbooks but only certain ones shine for you, it can be fun to use those pages in a scrapbook. Of course, it's fine to keep cookbooks that you really like as books, and I also have many of those. But if there are any cookbooks you don't use much or that don't seem to fit your current lifestyle, you can make your own original joy-filled recipe book by copying and compiling the recipes or photos you like.

By putting thought into which recipes truly spark joy, you can create a collection of meals that nourish not only your body but also your connection to others.

Spinach with sesame sauce

SERVES 4

1 tablespoon toasted white sesame seeds

Pinch of salt

180g fresh spinach

1½ teaspoons soy sauce

Spinach is rich in iron, and sesame seeds are antioxidants. Nutritious and easy to make, this dish is a staple of Japanese home cooking.

Grind the sesame seeds in a mortar and pestle or spice grinder.

Bring a medium pot of water to a boil over high heat and add the salt. Add the spinach and blanch for 45 to 60 seconds, until the spinach is bright green and just tender.

Drain the spinach in a colander and run it under cold water before it gets too soft. Squeeze out the excess water, cut the spinach into 5cm lengths, and place it in a serving dish.

In a small bowl, combine the ground sesame seeds and soy sauce. Pour the sesame sauce over the spinach and use tongs to mix it in. Serve immediately.

My mother's black vinegar chicken wing stew

SERVES 4

My mother often made this tasty, protein-packed recipe for me as a child. Now I continue the tradition and serve it frequently for my own family. If you don't have oyster sauce on hand, you can substitute additional black vinegar in its place.

Pour the 2 teaspoons of soy sauce into a shallow bowl. Pierce the skin on the wings here and there with a knife, then roll them in the soy sauce to flavour.

Heat the sesame oil in a large pot over medium heat. Add the ginger and garlic and sauté for 2 minutes, until fragrant. Add the chicken wings, in batches if necessary, and sauté for 2 to 3 minutes per side, until browned.

Meanwhile, in a bowl, combine the water, black vinegar, oyster sauce, the remaining 2 tablespoons of soy sauce, the sugar, and sake. Pour the mixture over the chicken wings in the pot and bring the sauce to a boil. Add the leek and carrot, reduce the heat to medium-low, and simmer, covered, for 20 minutes.

Sprinkle the wings with coriander and serve hot with rice.

Note: If using spring onions in place of the Japanese leek, stir them into the stew in the last few minutes of cooking.

2 tablespoons plus 2 teaspoons soy sauce

12 chicken wings

4 teaspoons sesame oil or olive oil

2.5cm piece unpeeled ginger, sliced into 4 disks

1 clove garlic, minced (optional)

950ml water

4 tablespoons black rice vinegar or vinegar of your choice

4 tablespoons oyster sauce

2 tablespoons sugar

2 tablespoons sake

1 Japanese leek or 1 bunch spring onions (see note), tender white and green parts, sliced on a diagonal into bite-size pieces (optional)

1 carrot, peeled and cut into bite-size chunks (optional)

1 tablespoon chopped coriander (optional)

Cooked white or brown rice, for serving

Discover the joy of fermentation.

I began making my own fermented foods, such as miso and amazake, fairly recently. The flavour is influenced not only by the type of rice, soya beans, and malted rice used, but also literally by the hands of the cook. The skin on our hands is home to indigenous beneficial bacteria. These bacteria may be more acidic or more alkaline, depending on the person, and it's why miso kneaded by hand tastes different – sometimes milder, sometimes stronger – depending on who made it, reflecting the individuality of the cook. That's one of the joys of making your own fermented food.

Countless bacteria live inside our bodies too, keeping our immune system well-tuned and adjusting imbalances when we're feeling sick or run down. The amino acids and vitamins in fermented foods help to activate our beneficial bacteria.

Why not take the time to appreciate your relationship with your own resident flora by making or eating fermented foods? When you think of them with gratitude, you'll come to appreciate your body even more.

Amazing amazake

MAKES 8 TO 10 SERVINGS

Amazake is a traditional fermented Japanese drink made with koji, or malted rice. It is mildly sweet and low in alcohol. Maintaining the right temperature is important for successful fermentation. If the mixture is too hot or too cold, the rice won't ferment, so take extra care with that step of the recipe – an electric pressure cooker or rice cooker will do the job – and be sure to have an instant thermometer on hand to help you maintain the temperature.

In a medium pot with a lid, bring the water to a boil over high heat. Add the rice, turn the heat to low, and simmer, covered, for 15 minutes, until the rice is soft and evenly cooked. Alternatively, if you have a rice cooker, use the okayu (porridge) setting.

Cool the rice porridge to a temperature between 55°C and 60°C and stir in the koji. (Remember: maintaining this temperature range is key.)

Place the mixture in an electric pressure cooker on low heat or a rice cooker set to warm and ferment for 8 hours, uncovered, until the amazake has sweetened and looks like rice porridge. During fermenting, stir the mixture and measure the temperature every 2 hours. Stir the mixture to lower the heat if the temperature is getting too high and cover the top of the cooker with a damp towel to prevent water from evaporating.

Serve warm or chilled in a small cup. Amazake will turn sour if it continues fermenting, so bring any leftovers to a boil to stop the fermentation process, then store in an airtight container in the refrigerator for up to 10 days.

1.9 litres water

400g Japanese white rice or mochi rice, rinsed

400g dried rice koji

Lessons from My Grandfather

As an acupuncturist, my grandfather treated sumo wrestlers, helping them to prevent and recover from injuries. He also appeared on TV shows, explaining the health benefits of pressing certain points in the ears and the soles of the feet. Perhaps not surprisingly, my mother was also a health nut and an avid follower of the latest wellness trends touted by books and on TV. Having grown up watching these two, I couldn't help but be influenced by them.

My mother would clip a clothespin to my ear, saying, 'If you stimulate this pressure point here, it will keep you sharp and improve your complexion too.' I listened, captivated. When I was in high school, taping your feet near the front of the arch was the latest health craze, and I eagerly tried it out. I don't know if it worked, but looking back on it, I realize the practice would have stimulated the pressure points in the sole of the foot, improving circulation.

My mother and grandfather also taught me a lot about healthy foods and cooking. My mother would make kefir and also boil vegetable scraps and strain them to make a very thin broth. Although the broth was bland and not at all tasty, I did feel a bit healthier when I drank it.

Acupressure and vegetable broth both improve the circulation of body fluids, which helps our intestines function well. To prevent constipation, I make sure to eat enough fiber and fermented foods and keep my liquid intake high. When our gut is working properly, it improves the circulation of fluids throughout the body.

One curious effect of tidying many clients have reported is that once they have purged their home of things that don't spark joy, their body will spontaneously purge their gut. There's no scientific basis upon which to draw a connection, and this could be due to some other factor like exposure to dust, but it is a phenomenon many clients mention. Our minds and bodies are connected, so while you're tidying, imagine that you're also cleansing your digestive system. You may find that your circulation improves and your complexion brightens.

Revel in an Inconvenient Lifestyle

In my profession, I see every fad in 'handy' household goods. Reusable silicon seals to replace plastic wrap, clips to close bags of food that have been opened, laundry rings that eliminate the need for detergent, potato chip makers, and so on. While some are improved upon until they become household standards, hundreds vanish as quickly as they appear because they're less handy than they seem.

Interestingly, in recent years, an increasing number of my clients seem to be pursuing the opposite of convenience, doing their own preserving and pickling – even making their own miso. Eating fermented foods has become another health boom after being rediscovered as a way to restore balance to our gut. Inspired by such clients, I began making my own miso (see page 126). It takes time, but the feeling of anticipation as I wait for each batch to be ready is always exhilarating.

This willingness to go to extra trouble to make something isn't limited to fermentation. I also have clients offering me home-cured bacon or homegrown carrots. Nor is this limited to food. Some of my clients have started using sanitary pads made of cloth, while others have taken up sewing again.

It seems that as my clients progress in the tidying process, the number of them who actively choose a *less* convenient lifestyle increases in inverse proportion to the reduction of not-so-useful 'handy' goods. And they are having fun!

The reason is quite clear. When you finish tidying, you have more time. In fact, the greatest change that happens at the end of a tidying festival is how people use their time. Not only do they need less time for vacuuming or choosing what to wear, but they also spend far less time searching for things and struggling to make decisions. The time formerly spent on these less-than-joyful tasks is now freed up. Putting one's home in order appears to foster a strong desire to live more mindfully.

A while back, I visited a couple who had finished their tidying festival a few years earlier. After tidying up, they moved out of Tokyo to raise their child in the country and try farming. 'Even though we no longer have a TV and gave up many things, our lives are far more satisfying,' they told me. They stopped to watch their four-year-old daughter happily pulling weeds in the garden. 'Actually,' one of them remarked, 'this might be the perfect environment for raising her to be "wise" in the true sense of the word. Not having everything teaches patience. It challenges the mind and reminds us to be thankful for small things.'

Take a mental retreat through relaxation and meditation.

Although I take time out to relax every morning, afternoon, and evening, with my current lifestyle raising small children, it's difficult to find time to meditate. When I was single, I could schedule meditation into my day, but now I meditate while I'm doing other things.

This could be while I'm out for a walk, doing stretches before bed, cleaning, or cooking. It's possible to meditate during all of these activities. I can clear my mind during any simple, repetitive act, like chopping vegetables for minestrone. All I need to do is focus fully on the task at hand. When any thoughts or feelings pop into my head, I let them go without latching onto them.

Japanese Buddhist priests view temple chores, such as cleaning, as a form of meditation practice. Such tasks can be done without thinking. Focusing on the movements makes it possible to empty the mind of distracting thoughts.

By including in your daily routine moments when you can clear your mind, you can gradually increase the amount of time you spend meditating each day.

Look forward to your evening ritual.

As a university student, I was always pursuing the latest bedtime craze. Magazine articles advocated things like face massage, stretching exercises, or yoga before bed, and I followed all these tips religiously, never missing a day. Even then I was a perfectionist. If I was going to try something, I had to do it 'quickly, thoroughly, all in one go'. But once I graduated and began working for a company, I became so busy that things began to slip. I frequently fell asleep with my makeup on, or worse yet, would doze off on the floor or with my face pressed against my computer.

Through trial and error, gradually I have found an ideal bedtime routine that suits my life. Now that I'm married and raising children, it usually goes something like this: After our family meal, I put the children to bed at 7:30 with some bedtime stories. My husband usually goes to bed at the same time. Since much of his work involves communicating with people in Japan, he often has to get up before 4:00 in the morning. Once everyone else is asleep, it's my turn to relax. I tidy up the kitchen, prepare food for the following day, check my email, and draw up the next day's schedule. Then I make myself a cup of tea and reflect on my day. When I notice things I should be grateful for or things I would like to do differently or improve on, I jot them down in my notebook.

Being a morning person, I don't have a fixed bedtime routine. I might diffuse some essential oil and apply some skin-care products. Sometimes I'll add in some stretches as well to loosen up my body. My goal is simply to relax so I can get a good night's sleep, and what I need will vary depending on the day.

Rather than following a set ritual, I pay more attention to what *not* to do. For example, I avoid things that stimulate the autonomic nervous system, such as cold drinks or going online.

If I have extra time, I take a nice, long soak in the tub. In Japan, our tubs are deep, and we usually soak in them once a day. It's an efficient way to heat up your whole body so it can relax. As Japanese homes are often too small to allow much privacy, bath time is also a rare chance to enjoy being alone, which makes it extra special. Just taking the time to savour your bath by adding your favourite bath salts or lighting candles in the room can wash away fatigue and help you sleep soundly. Or, if you're the type who takes a bath in the morning, it gives you a chance to cleanse both your body and mind so you can start your day feeling renewed.

Customs and conditions vary widely from one region and country to another. In some places, water is scarce and expensive, and people conserve it carefully. Since I moved to America, I no longer have a bath every day, and instead will take a shower or soak my feet in a footbath. Being able to change those elements that bring you joy to suit the place you live is one of the charms of experiencing other ways of life.

Whether you prefer a bath or a shower, the purpose is the same: cleanliness. In Japan, cleansing the body is seen as an act of purification that not only washes away physical dirt, but also all the negative thoughts and pent-up feelings that have accumulated during the day. Regardless of the form it takes, it is a custom I value.

A good evening ritual can help us to awake feeling refreshed, almost reborn. The core of our being will seem to have clicked back into its rightful place – as when every possession fits perfectly into its designated storage spot. It's as if our mind has been put in order while we slept. We may be greeted by a flash of insight that solves a nagging problem or the realization that it's a waste of time to worry at all. For me, aromatherapy, yoga, and bathing before bed all have this same revitalizing effect.

When we wake in the morning with our heart and mind refreshed, it's so much easier to choose the actions that will make our day just right. In that sense, bedtime may be the most crucial part of the day for attaining our ideal lifestyle.

Wear only cotton or silk pyjamas.

When we tidy by choosing only those things we love, we dramatically increase our sensitivity to joy. By this, I simply mean that we hone our five senses. Tidying in this way makes us far more aware of what we enjoy in terms of taste, smell, touch, sight, and sound. Repeatedly asking ourselves whether something sparks joy sharpens these innate human faculties.

Of the five senses, smell and touch evolve the most markedly. Of course, the tidying process also develops our sense of sight. For one thing, it dramatically reduces the volume of objects cluttering our line of vision, which makes it easier to see the things we don't need. And as we think about how to arrange our storage attractively, we refine our appreciation for visual beauty. Our sense of sight, however, is already well honed because it's what humans use the most in making decisions. That's why the greatest developmental leap occurs in our senses of smell and touch.

Which brings me to the main topic. The reason I believe tidying particularly sharpens these two senses is because I've noticed that my clients become very particular about materials once they've tidied up. For example, the number of clothes made from synthetic materials in their wardrobe drops, and they start choosing cloth bags over plastic ones. As their sensitivity to joy rises, they gravitate toward things that feel good against the skin (their sense of touch) and that create a pleasant atmosphere (their sense of smell).

By the word *atmosphere*, I don't mean just fragrances, like incense. Our sense of smell detects something more fundamental – essences in the air that shape the mood within the home. For example, wooden objects exude tranquility and ease; steel, a dignified coolness; and plastic, a bustling clatter. The nature of the air that pervades your home is determined by the materials within it. And it is your sense of smell that is the most sensitive to any variations.

That's why I'm very particular about the pyjamas I wear. I insist on using 100 per cent silk or cotton. As silk is very hard to get, the reality is that most of my pyjamas are cotton. Nowadays, I almost exclusively use pyjamas made from a soft organic cotton that is gentler on both the environment and the skin.

The only time we can escape from our thoughts and completely relax is when we're asleep. If we want to pursue comfort, the best way is to invest in the hours we spend sleeping. For me, inspirations and solutions to problems usually come the moment I wake up in the morning. Perhaps getting a deep, rejuvenating sleep awakens the sixth sense, which transcends the other five.

Browse through a joy scrapbook before bed.

As a child, I used to dream of curling up in bed with a favourite photo album or a lovely art catalog. I imagined browsing through the pages and sipping herbal tea until I nodded off to sleep. Perhaps this image was influenced by something I saw in a movie or magazine. To realize this dream though, I had to find a book with beautiful pictures or photos, which was actually quite difficult. I searched all over for one that seemed just right, checking out fashionable interior decorating magazines at the library and buying photo books of other countries.

Eventually, at an exhibition, I stumbled across a catalog of dishes used by Queen Victoria. Its delightful images captivated me as I turned the pages – plates with exquisite floral designs, a teapot with a bird-shaped knob on its lid, and teacups with elegant blue patterns. Having been to the exhibition, I could picture the dishes each time I turned the pages and was enchanted all over again.

There was one problem, however. Art catalogs are large and awkward, and heavier than a dictionary. Holding it on my lap in bed made my solar plexus ache within minutes. I couldn't possibly nod off while reading. And if I spread the book open on my bed and lay on my stomach, I would likely spill my tea. What was I to do?

After taking a closer look at the catalog, I realized that more than half of its two hundred or so pages were devoted to explanations, and half of those were written in English, which I couldn't understand at the time. In fact, the number of pages that actually brought me joy was surprisingly limited. Only five or six photos really fascinated me. So, I cut out only those pages that sparked joy and pasted them into a scrapbook with an antique-style chocolate-brown cover I particularly loved. The result was beyond my expectations.

Since then, I have continued to cut out pictures or photographs that I like from other books to paste in this scrapbook. I choose only those that really bring me joy. For example, if I love a pair of shoes worn by a model in a photo, I cut out just the shoes. Of course, if the book is in good condition and can be sold or donated, there is no need to tackle it with a pair of scissors. The photos you love can be colour copied instead. The point is not to hang onto things that don't spark joy. Just make sure you don't overlook any photos that do bring joy before you bid the book farewell. (And if the whole book brings you joy, of course you should keep it!)

If a photo grabs me when I'm reading a magazine at the hairdresser, I'll jot down the name and the issue and pick up a copy. Out of ten magazines, I'm lucky to find even one photo that speaks to me in this way. Which goes to show how rare and precious such an encounter is. In my experience, when we recognize and appreciate the little joys in our lives, we're more likely to encounter the big ones.

Incidentally, the contents of my scrapbook are organized by colour. When I need a pick-me-up, I open it to the orange page. When I want to relax, I look at the collection of green items. I also have a page devoted to cakes and Japanese desserts that I turn to when I crave something sweet. (This may be the one I look at most frequently!) When a particular picture no longer brings me joy, I don't hesitate to rip it out and paste in a new one that does.

Thanks to my joy scrapbook, I have realized my childhood dream of curling up in bed with a cup of tea and a book of gorgeous pictures. If this idea appeals to you, consider investing in your own special collection – and always keep your eyes peeled for images that spark joy for you.

The life-changing magic of a daily gratitude practice.

I pray every night before I go to sleep. Or perhaps *prayer* is too formal a word. I simply express gratitude in my mind. When I first started out, I vaguely imagined I was talking to God or the spirits of my ancestors, but gradually, concrete images of familiar things and people came to mind.

Now I begin by thanking my pajamas, and expand outward to include my bed, my bedroom, and my home, thanking each thing around me. Next, I move on to my husband, my children, my parents, my siblings, my grandparents on both sides, their parents, and beyond them to ancestors I don't even know, all of them branching outward from me on our family tree. When I do this, gratitude wells up inside me. I'm profoundly grateful just for being here in this moment and for always being held and protected within something far greater. My body feels lighter, and I drift off to sleep.

By adding a nightly gratitude practice to your routine, whether it's journaling or focusing your mind as you lie in bed, you can discard the weight of your troubles. Remembering what you are grateful for puts your life in perspective and hones your sense of joy and appreciation for all the blessings in your life.

Practise Accepting Gifts Graciously

People who are good at gift giving are wonderful, aren't they? I'm the opposite. I even went through a phase where I stopped giving any presents at all. I celebrated special occasions by sending a card, and when I did give a gift, I limited myself to impermanent things like flowers or food. I worried that if I gave something that lasted, it might just burden the receiver, and the thought that it would be thrown away some day made me sad.

Perhaps this 'gift-giving phobia' stemmed from seeing my clients agonize over whether to dispose of gifts that sparked no joy and from witnessing the distressing arguments that arose whenever someone committed the cardinal sin of discarding a gift in front of the giver.

Of course, I avoided accumulating unnecessary items, and always politely declined when clients invited me to take anything I wanted from the things they had chosen not to keep.

My former secretary, Kaori, is similar. She's good at tidying and avoids accumulating extraneous things. So, for her birthday, I always asked her what she wanted or gave her something practical like coupons for rice. This changed, however, when she got engaged. I wanted to do something different to celebrate the special occasion of her marriage and decided to give her something handmade, which is number one

on the list of unwelcome gifts. To make sure it would be welcome, I consulted with the rest of the staff, and together we decided to make her a heart-shaped potholder. Each person was assigned a task, such as purchasing the cloth, making the base, embroidering it, and beading it, and when each person finished, they passed the potholder onto the next person. I was responsible for the embroidery, and, to my surprise, I enjoyed it so much that I became totally engrossed in the work.

As my needle wove back and forth through the cloth, picking out Kaori's favourite words in thread, I realized that tidying up had made me feel guilty about acquiring more possessions. Likewise, when it came to giving a special person a gift, I worried about causing them trouble instead of focusing on my desire to make them happy.

My taboo about gift giving melted away at the sight of Kaori's radiant face, and I now give gifts more often. It's actually a wonderful thing to do. Interestingly, I also began to receive more gifts from others, which is also wonderful. Some people tease me, saying, 'I bet when you get a gift, you thank it for the joy of receiving it and then throw it away.' But that's not true. Perhaps because I've already let go of so much in my life, I like to make good use of the gifts I receive.

I display various ornaments I receive immediately. When someone drew a portrait of me, I hung it on the wall then and there, and any gifts of tea or sweets are shared with my staff within three days. When I come across an unopened gift in a client's house, I give them the homework of using it by our next lesson. One of my clients used new dishes each time I visited, which made every lesson into a classy tea party.

There's just one rule for effectively using presents: unwrap them, remove them from the box, and start using them as soon as you receive them.

Sometimes I'm asked what we should do if we receive something that doesn't spark joy, but there's no need to worry. Strangely enough, everything received after we finish our tidying festival seems to inspire joy; very few gifts spark no joy at all. If you do receive something that doesn't click right away, try using it. It may seem odd to 'force' yourself to use it, but through tidying up you have honed your sense of the things you own and the things you like. You now have the emotional space to try out something new and to enjoy things that are different.

There's no rule that you have to use a gift forever, and if, after a short while, it seems to have fulfilled its purpose, then it's time to let it go. By then, you should be able to do so guilt-free and with sincere gratitude.

To tell the truth, I have only recently gained this degree of flexibility. Tidying up hones our ability to actively select what we want to keep from what we already own. Perhaps that fact made me overlook the ability to simply accept what I receive. Learning to graciously accept the kindness of others has made my life much easier.

It may sound like an exaggeration, but I feel that making good use of gifts helps me to take advantage of opportunities that come my way, as if I'm opening myself up to receive good fortune. It's a waste not to use a gift that someone has gone to the trouble of giving us. There is always meaning in our encounters with things. Using the gifts we are given can lead to the discovery of some unexpected joy that wasn't apparent at first sight.

CONCLUSION

Live a joyful life with what you have now.

K's notion of the ideal lifestyle was having a home where she could spend time enjoying meals with friends and family. I'm sure many of us share her dream.

'I know people who invite their friends over for parties,' K told me, 'but I've never been able to do that, even though I'd love to. I have to tidy up before it's possible.' Her tidying progressed quickly. Around the time she finished tidying her papers, we took a break, and she brought out some buns she had picked up at a nearby bakery. During my tidying lessons I often plow straight through without any breaks, so I'm grateful when my clients offer me something to eat. In this case, however, she merely plunked down the buns, still in their wrappers, along with some drinks in plastic bottles. 'Here,' she said. 'Take your pick.' This seemed to be disrespectful of good food and a waste of the time we were taking to eat it.

We haven't tidied the kitchen yet, I thought. *Still, she must have some dishes that spark joy.* With her permission, I opened her cupboard, only to see an amazing array of beautiful tableware! I took out two lovely floral plates stacked in the back of the cupboard that seemed to be crying out, 'Use me! Use me!' I warmed up the buns in the oven and arranged them on the plates. Then I poured the bottled tea into some beautiful Edo-Kiriko glasses that K had never removed from their paulownia wood box. The result? In just a few minutes, our break was transformed into an elegant little luncheon.

The point I'm trying to make is this: we can realize many elements of our ideal lifestyle right now just by using what's already at hand. Do you think only people who have nice dishes and a tidy kitchen can enjoy a beautiful lifestyle? Well, that's simply not true. With a little ingenuity, creativity, and playfulness, anyone can make their life joyful with what they already have. There are so many ways to do this.

One is to celebrate seasonal occasions. When I was a child, my mother loved events of all kinds – there was never a month when she couldn't find something to celebrate. This included not only traditional Japanese festivals such as Tanabata, the Star Festival, but also holidays from other cultures, such as Halloween. Only instead of making pumpkin jack-o'-lanterns, we drew felt-pen faces on tangerines – easier to find in Japan than big orange pumpkins – and placed one in every room. In December, we put up a little Christmas tree in the hall and decorated it. Turkeys are also hard to get in Japan, so on Christmas Eve my mother bought a roasted chicken at the local supermarket and tied cute ribbons around the tips of the drumsticks.

When I want decorations that reflect the season, I often hang up tenugui, traditional Japanese cotton hand towels with attractive designs, in the entranceway or living room. Rather than decorating the whole house, I hang only one or two of these in strategic spots, such as in the dining room for the family to enjoy when we gather for meals or in the front hall. While I only stick these cloth prints to the wall with removable adhesive tape, they change the atmosphere as completely as if I had changed the wallpaper. When I exchange one tenugui for another to depict the next season, it's my family and the many things we have done together that I recall. Although these are just simple memories of an ordinary family, to me they're priceless.

When we put our home in order, it changes our lives. For many, that change is dramatic. But even when the change isn't dramatic, it's wonderful to learn how to savour each moment of our lives.

I hope that through the magic of tidying up, your life and your home will spark joy for you every day.

AFTERWORD

While I was writing this book, we welcomed our third child, a son, into our family. This is my first time raising a boy, and it brings with it new surprises and challenges. The addition of a new family member has caused significant changes in my schedule, and I'm much busier at the moment. We've acquired a few more things, the layout of our house has changed, and the way we use our time is a little different too.

I'm sure that with each new stage in our lives – like when the children grow and move on to higher grades, when we move to a new home, or when our work changes – my vision of an ideal kurashi, or lifestyle, my priorities in life, and my concept of joyful ways to use time will also change. The lifestyle I've described here reflects what gives me joy at this particular stage in my life.

People sometimes tell me that the things that used to bring them joy no longer do. This is perfectly natural. What sparks joy for you will change. What's important is the process of examining what brings you joy each time it changes. Be attuned to your sense of joy at every moment of your life, and rejoice in each day you spend with those you love. It would give me the greatest happiness if this book helped you do that.

With joy and gratitude,

Marie Kondo

YOUR IDEAL LIFESTYLE WORKSHEETS

Self-reflection is a crucial part of the tidying process. Tidying helps you discover what is important to you and what you truly value in life – and it's this knowledge that prevents rebounding to clutter. The pages that follow will help you reflect on and discover yourself as you carry out your tidying festival.

Grab your favourite notebook and start jotting down thoughts on 'your ideal lifestyle', things you notice while tidying, and changes you experience through the process. Many people use a computer or smartphone to take notes, but I recommend writing things down by hand. It's much easier to organize your thoughts and see things clearly when writing longhand than when typing.

For example, I usually jot down things that spark joy for me that day or thoughts that come to mind. This habit helps me identify what activities bring me the most joy and what kind of possessions give me a sense of fulfilment.

Tidying is a great opportunity for self-reflection and self-discovery. Use these worksheets to get in touch with your inner self, create a tidy home, and realize your ideal lifestyle. To make it easy, I've outlined all the necessary steps in this section.

Visualize your ideal morning.

Write down your ideal morning schedule starting from the moment you wake up until you leave the house or begin your work day. What's the first thing you'd like to do? Be specific. Visualize yourself actually doing each activity, such as relaxing with a cup of tea or vacuuming the floor. Then picture what you need to do and what state your home needs to be in to make this possible. You'll realize how important it is to have tidied up!

Sample Timeline

Write down what you need to do to achieve your ideal morning, such as 'Clear the floor for stretching'.

If you work from home or are the main caregiver or homemaker of your family, this part of your morning is from the time you wake up until you begin your work or tasks. If you work or study outside the home, it's from the time you wake up until you walk out the door.

Include a joy-sparking activity to kick-start a great day. Be as specific as possible. Jotting down the details makes your ideal easier to attain.

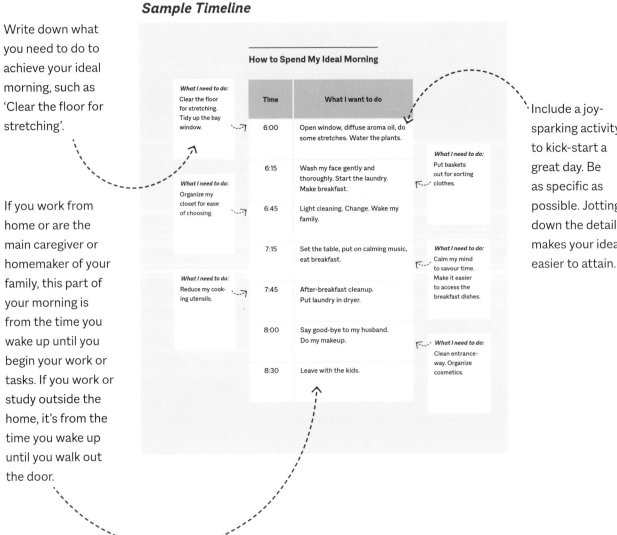

How to Spend My Ideal Morning

Time	What I want to do
6:00	Open window, diffuse aroma oil, do some stretches. Water the plants.
6:15	Wash my face gently and thoroughly. Start the laundry. Make breakfast.
6:45	Light cleaning. Change. Wake my family.
7:15	Set the table, put on calming music, eat breakfast.
7:45	After-breakfast cleanup. Put laundry in dryer.
8:00	Say good-bye to my husband. Do my makeup.
8:30	Leave with the kids.

What I need to do:
Clear the floor for stretching. Tidy up the bay window.

What I need to do:
Organize my closet for ease of choosing.

What I need to do:
Reduce my cooking utensils.

What I need to do:
Put baskets out for sorting clothes.

What I need to do:
Calm my mind to savour time. Make it easier to access the breakfast dishes.

What I need to do:
Clean entrance-way. Organize cosmetics.

How to Spend My Ideal Morning

What I need to do:

What I need to do:

What I need to do:

What I need to do:

Time	What I want to do

What I need to do:

What I need to do:

What I need to do:

Visualize your ideal day.

Just as for your ideal morning, draw up an ideal timeline for how you want to spend your day. Give thought to how you can create the conditions you need to realize your ideal, such as by listening to podcasts to calm your mind or using audio books to learn a new language or skill during your commute. Be sure to include time for self-care and pursuing your interests, walking or exercising, seeing friends, picking up and playing with your kids, household chores, shopping, and tidying. Through this process, you will clearly identify what you want to do and what you need to do, making it easy and natural to find time to spark joy.

Sample Timeline

Visualize the flow of your day, and write down what needs to be done before you leave home or start a task. This will give you more time to spare during the day.

Be sure to include joyful moments in your schedule, such as being with family, so that you keep your thoughts consciously focused on making time to spark joy.

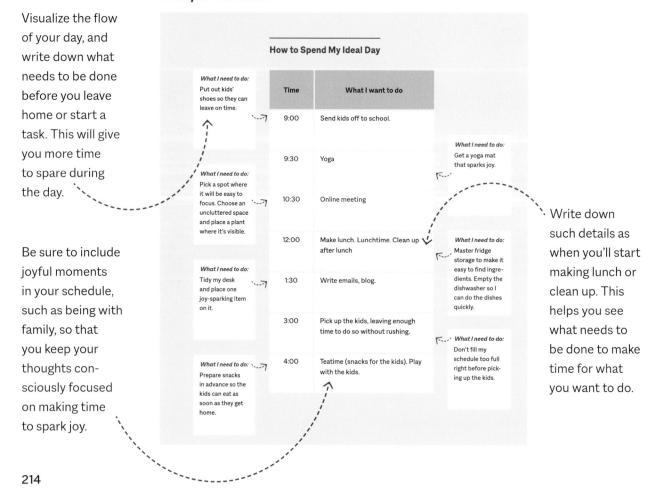

How to Spend My Ideal Day

What I need to do:
Put out kids' shoes so they can leave on time.

What I need to do:
Pick a spot where it will be easy to focus. Choose an uncluttered space and place a plant where it's visible.

What I need to do:
Tidy my desk and place one joy-sparking item on it.

What I need to do:
Prepare snacks in advance so the kids can eat as soon as they get home.

Time	What I want to do
9:00	Send kids off to school.
9:30	Yoga
10:30	Online meeting
12:00	Make lunch. Lunchtime. Clean up after lunch
1:30	Write emails, blog.
3:00	Pick up the kids, leaving enough time to do so without rushing.
4:00	Teatime (snacks for the kids). Play with the kids.

What I need to do:
Get a yoga mat that sparks joy.

What I need to do:
Master fridge storage to make it easy to find ingredients. Empty the dishwasher so I can do the dishes quickly.

What I need to do:
Don't fill my schedule too full right before picking up the kids.

Write down such details as when you'll start making lunch or clean up. This helps you see what needs to be done to make time for what you want to do.

_____

How to Spend My Ideal Day

Time	What I want to do

What I need to do:

What I need to do:

What I need to do:

What I need to do:

What I need to do:

What I need to do:

What I need to do:

Visualize your ideal evening.

Think about your ideal way of spending your time when you come home from work, school, or errands. This includes right up to when you go to bed. How you spend this period of the day influences the quality of your sleep and how you feel when you wake up the next morning. That's why we should carefully consider how to avoid overstimulation and instead organize our living environment for optimum relaxation, creating both the time and space to wind down.

Sample Timeline

Imagine what kind of environment you need to feel a sense of ease and relief. This will help you identify what you need to do to achieve your ideal evening, such as 'keeping the table clear of clutter'.

Just before bed, focus your thoughts on gratitude for your family and all those who are close to you, as well as for that day. This resets your heart and mind so you wake refreshed.

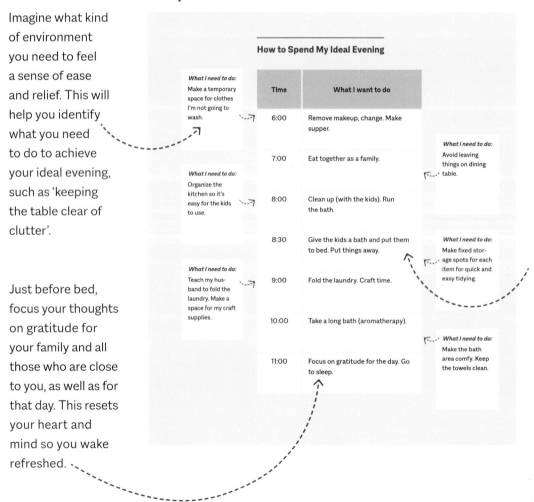

How to Spend My Ideal Evening

What I need to do:	Time	What I want to do
Make a temporary space for clothes I'm not going to wash.	6:00	Remove makeup, change. Make supper.
	7:00	Eat together as a family.
Organize the kitchen so it's easy for the kids to use.	8:00	Clean up (with the kids). Run the bath.
	8:30	Give the kids a bath and put them to bed. Put things away.
Teach my husband to fold the laundry. Make a space for my craft supplies.	9:00	Fold the laundry. Craft time.
	10:00	Take a long bath (aromatherapy).
	11:00	Focus on gratitude for the day. Go to sleep.

What I need to do: Avoid leaving things on dining table.

What I need to do: Make fixed storage spots for each item for quick and easy tidying.

What I need to do: Make the bath area comfy. Keep the towels clean.

Picture what you want to do to prepare for the next day and ensure a good night's rest from the time you come home until you go to bed. Don't pack too much into your evening.

How to Spend My Ideal Evening

Time	What I want to do

What I need to do:

What I need to do:

What I need to do:

What I need to do:

What I need to do:

What I need to do:

What I need to do:

Spend a relaxing evening.

ACKNOWLEDGEMENTS

I am immensely grateful to everyone who helped produce this book, including developmental editor Lisa Westmoreland, who was involved from the planning phase; editor Julie Bennett and art director Betsy Stromberg from Ten Speed Press; my agent Neil Gudovitz; Tomoko Ishibashi for her editorial collaboration with the Japanese manuscript; The Outset team for their beautiful photography; Leanne Citrone for kindly letting us use her gorgeous home for one of the photoshoots; and Cathy Hirano for translating the manuscript. And many thanks to Kay Amano for her skillful coordination, tireless support, and enthusiasm.

And finally, a heartfelt thanks to you for choosing this book.

Wishing you a life that sparks joy every day!

INDEX

First published in the United States by Ten Speed Press, an imprint of Random House,
a division of Penguin Random House LLC, New York

This edition first published in the UK 2022 by Bluebird, an imprint of Pan Macmillan
The Smithson, 6 Briset Street, London EC1M 5NR
EU representative: Macmillan Publishers Ireland Ltd, 1st Floor, The Liffey Trust Centre,
117–126 Sheriff Street Upper, Dublin 1, D01 YC43
Associated companies throughout the world
www.panmacmillan.com

ISBN 978-1-5290-8509-9

Portions of this book were originally published in Japan as *Mainichi ga tokimeku katazuke
no mahō* (*Spark Joy Every Day*) by Sunmark Shuppan, Tokyo, in 2014.

9 8 7 6 5 4 3 2 1

A CIP catalogue record for this book is available from the British Library.

Printed and bound in Spain

Visit **www.panmacmillan.com** to read more about all our books and to buy them. You will
also find features, author interviews and news of any author events, and you can sign up
for e-newsletters so that you're always first to hear about our new releases.